The Galveston Diet Cookbook with Color Pictures for Beginners

The Galveston Diet Cookbook with Color Pictures for Beginners

96 No-Stress Anti-Inflammatory Recipes to Balance Hormones, Burn Fat and Reduce Uncomfortable Menopausal & Perimenopausal Symptoms

Brant Grenier

Contents

A short message from the author

Hey there! How's the book treating you? I'm super curious to know what you think about it!

You know, reviews can be a total game-changer for authors. They're like gold but harder to find! Your thoughts can really make a difference.

Could you spare just a minute to jot down a quick review on Amazon? Even a few sentences would mean the world!

Simply click the link 🔗 or scan the QR code below to leave your review on Amazon

🔗 https://mybook.to/galvestoncolorcookbook

QR code

Thank you for taking the time to share your thoughts!

Your review will genuinely make a difference for me and help me gain exposure for my work.

Brant Grenier

INTRODUCTION

In the ever-evolving landscape of health and nutrition, the *Galveston diet* emerges as a beacon of change, specifically designed for perimenopausal and menopausal women navigating the intricacies of their changing bodies. Rooted in the growing realm of anti-inflammatory diets, the Galveston diet not only stands as a testament to the importance of mindful nutrition but also introduces a unique blend of intermittent fasting, anti-inflammatory principles, and strategic nutritional shifts.

At its core, the *Galveston diet* draws inspiration from well-established anti-inflammatory diets like the Mediterranean and DASH diets. Crafted with precision, it encompasses three key components: intermittent fasting, an anti-inflammatory nutritional approach, and a personalized shift in nutritional intake. This holistic framework aims not only to promote overall health but also addresses the specific challenges faced by women during perimenopause and menopause.

A standout feature of the Galveston diet is the incorporation of 16:8 intermittent fasting, where individuals consume their meals within an eight-hour window, followed by a 16-hour fasting period. This approach not only fosters metabolic flexibility but also aligns with the diet's overarching goal of mitigating inflammation. By restricting processed foods, added sugars, and inflammatory ingredients, the diet emphasizes a profound connection between nutrition and overall well-being.

While the Galveston diet shares common ground with the Keto diet, particularly in its high-fat, low-carb phase, it distinguishes itself in crucial aspects. Unlike the sustained low-carb approach of Keto, the Galveston diet gradually increases carb intake after an initial phase, reflecting a nuanced understanding of nutritional needs. Furthermore, the Galveston diet meticulously guides individuals on the types of fats to consume, highlighting the importance of healthy fats while excluding inflammatory counterparts.

In essence, the Galveston diet transcends the boundaries of a traditional diet, offering a strategic roadmap for women to navigate the complexities of hormonal changes with resilience, empowering them on their journey to enhanced well-being. This may feel like a niche diet or a concept that can't help you if you're not in this category, but according to Amy Fischer, MS, RD, CDN, a registered dietitian working within the Good Housekeeping Institute, it's one we should pay attention to regardless.

We all know that weight management doesn't have a one size fits all solution, and that many popular diets may not take your unique challenges into account, including your age. It's why experts are buzzing about a new category of diet advice entirely, and the Galveston diet, which has emerged as one of the best diet. Endorsed by nutritionists and dietitians alike, the Galveston diet with Its nuanced approach, pays equal attention to both the quality and quantity of food, setting it apart from conventional diets.

History of the Diet

Dr. Mary Claire Haver, a Texas-based OB-GYN, led the emergence of the Galveston diet, a revolutionary and personalized eating plan. She made this unique way of eating based on her own experiences during a time in her life when her body was changing a lot. Dr. Haver wanted to find a way to feel better and navigate the challenges that happen when hormones change in the body.

Dr. Haver's story starts in Galveston, Texas, where her body was going through changes because of her age. She had a hard time with her weight after her brother passed away, and during perimenopause. She wanted to not only lose weight but also understand how food, hormones, and health are connected.

Dr. Haver's special way of eating, called the Galveston diet, is different from regular diets. She doesn't see it as a quick fix but more like a way to eat for your whole life. She calls it a "lifetime eating plan." This way of eating helped her not only lose weight but also made her feel better during menopause, dealing with things like hot flashes and brain fog. It's like a helpful guide for women going through this big change in life.

At first, Dr. Haver tried the usual idea of "eat less, move more" to lose weight, which is something doctors often learn. But even when she really tried by eating less and exercising a lot, she didn't lose weight. This was surprising and different from what she expected.

Dr. Haver then looked into how food works in the body. She didn't just want to know how many calories she ate; she also wanted to know if the kind of food she ate was good. She talked to experts who told her that inflammation, something that happens inside our bodies, might be a reason why she couldn't lose weight, especially as people get older. This discovery made her think differently, not just about how much food she ate, but about the kind of food she ate.

The Galveston diet Is based on the idea that keeping your hormones in balance is really important for managing your weight. Dr. Haver, who created the diet, figured out that just focusing on the number of calories you eat and burn (like the traditional way) isn't enough. The diet says that the kind of food you eat affects your hormones, and that's a big deal.

In 2017, Dr. Haver shared the Galveston diet with everyone. It came from her own experiences and what she knew as a doctor. At first, she made it to help herself lose weight. But soon, it became a popular program that many people followed.

The Galveston diet is not just about losing weight; it's like a helpful guide for women going through menopause. Dr. Haver wants women to know it's more than a diet—it's a way of living that can last a long time. It helps women find balance in what they eat, their hormones, and their overall health.

The Diet Principles

The diet has three main parts: intermittent fasting, eating anti-inflammatory foods, and adjusting the balance of fats, proteins, and carbs in your meals.

Intermittent Fasting

The diet recommends a specific type of intermittent fasting called 16/8, where you fast for 16 hours and eat during an 8-hour window each day. This can create a calorie deficit, helping with weight loss. During the fasting hours, you can drink zero-calorie beverages like water, unsweetened tea, or coffee.

Anti-Inflammatory Foods

The Galveston diet focuses on eating foods that reduce inflammation in the body. This means avoiding processed foods, added sugars, and inflammatory items like fried foods. Instead, the plan encourages whole foods like fruits, vegetables, lentils, complex carbs, and lean meats.

High in Fat, Low in Carbs

Similar to the keto diet, the Galveston diet is high in healthy fats and low in carbs. In the beginning, about 70% of your daily calories come from fats, 20% from proteins, and 9% from carbs. This shift in energy sourcing aims to promote fat burning for weight loss. Over time, the diet adjusts, allowing for more complex carbs once your body gets used to eating fewer carbs and sugars.

What You Can Eat

Fruits (lower in sugar): Enjoy the sweetness of strawberries, blueberries, and raspberries.

Vegetables (low in starch): Incorporate greens, tomatoes, cucumbers, celery, zucchini, and broccoli.

Lean Proteins: Opt for chicken, salmon, tuna, turkey, and eggs.

Legumes: Include beans (chickpeas, black beans), lentils, and nuts/seeds (walnuts, almonds, chia seeds).

Whole Grains: Embrace the goodness of whole wheat bread, brown rice, quinoa, barley, oats, and buckwheat.

Dairy: Choose milk, yogurt, and cheese for a dose of calcium.

Healthy Fats: Include olive oil and avocado oil to support overall well-being.

Probiotic-Rich Additions: Include tea and fermented foods rich in probiotics for gut health.

Below is a detailed breakdown of what you can eat on the Galveston diet, organized into categories. It's important to note that the Galveston diet focuses on whole, nutrient-dense foods while limiting processed carbohydrates and sugars.

Category	What to Eat	Notes/Recommendations
Proteins	Lean meats (chicken, turkey, fish)	Choose high-quality, lean sources of protein.
	Eggs	Include both whole eggs and egg whites.
	Plant-based proteins (tofu, legumes)	Incorporate a variety of plant-based protein sources.
	Dairy products (Greek yogurt, cottage cheese)	Opt for low-fat or non-fat options.
Healthy Fats	Avocados	Rich in monounsaturated fats.
	Nuts and seeds (almonds, walnuts, chia seeds)	Great sources of omega-3 fatty acids.
	Olive oil	Use for cooking or as a salad dressing.
Vegetables	Leafy greens (spinach, kale, lettuce)	High in vitamins and minerals.
	Cruciferous vegetables (broccoli, cauliflower)	Supportive of hormonal balance.

	Colorful vegetables (bell peppers, tomatoes)	Provide a variety of antioxidants.
Fruits	Berries (blueberries, strawberries)	Low in sugar and high in antioxidants.
	Citrus fruits (oranges, grapefruits)	Rich in vitamin C.
Whole Grains	Quinoa	A nutrient-dense alternative to refined grains.
	Brown rice	Higher in fiber and nutrients than white rice.
Herbs and Spices	Turmeric	Known for its anti-inflammatory properties.
	Cinnamon	Adds flavor without added sugars.
Dairy Alternatives	Almond milk, coconut milk	Unsweetened varieties are preferred.
Condiments and Sauces	Olive oil-based dressings	Avoid dressings with added sugars or excessive fats.
	Mustard	Low-calorie option for flavor.

What You can't Eat

Pro-Inflammatory Foods: Steer clear of white flour, found in white bread, muffins, cookies, cakes, crackers, and pretzels.

Added Sugars: Say no to sodas, desserts, and syrups with high fructose corn syrup.

Alcohol: Restrict beer, wine, and liquor intake for better results.

Fried Foods: Avoid French fries and fried chicken sandwiches.

Vegetable Oils: Cut out canola or vegetable oil to reduce inflammatory impact.

Sweetened Treats: Say goodbye to sweetened yogurts, sugary cereals, cookies, candies, and processed meats (salami, bacon, sausage).

Limit Processed Foods: Minimize processed foods, added sugar, and alcohol.

The Galveston diet restricts certain foods that may contribute to inflammation, hormonal imbalances, or interfere with the overall goals of the diet. Below is a table detailing what to avoid on the Galveston diet:

Category	What to Avoid	Notes/Alternatives
Processed Carbohydrates	White bread and refined grains	Opt for whole grains like quinoa, brown rice, and oats.
	Sugary cereals and pastries	Choose breakfast options with low added sugars.
Added Sugars	Candy, sweets, and sugary snacks	Satisfy sweet cravings with fruits or limited natural sweeteners.
	Sugar-sweetened beverages	Opt for water, herbal teas, or unsweetened alternatives.
Processed Foods	Fast food and heavily processed meals	Focus on whole, minimally processed foods for nutrient density.
	Pre-packaged snacks and chips	Snack on nuts, seeds, or fresh fruits for healthier options.
Unhealthy Fats	Trans fats (partially hydrogenated oils)	Choose sources of healthy fats like avocados and nuts.
	Fried foods	Opt for baked, grilled, or sauteed cooking methods.
Dairy	Full-fat dairy products	Choose low-fat or non-fat options for dairy consumption.
Highly Processed Meats	Processed meats (sausages, hot dogs)	Opt for lean, unprocessed meats like chicken or turkey.
Highly Processed Beverages	Soda and sugary drinks	Prioritize water, herbal teas, or black coffee in moderation.
Highly Refined Oils	Vegetable oils high in omega-6 (soybean, corn oil)	Use healthier cooking oils like olive oil or coconut oil.
Excessive Caffeine	Excessive coffee or energy drinks	Limit caffeine intake and choose decaffeinated options.
Alcohol	Excessive alcohol consumption	Moderate alcohol intake; choose red wine for

		potential health benefits.
Artificial Additives	Artificial sweeteners, colors, and preservatives	Opt for natural sweeteners like stevia and whole foods.

Benefits of the Diet

In this section, we will talk about the numerous advantages of following this diet and highlighting aspects that may make it a compelling choice. Here are the advantages of the Galveston diet:

1. The diet emphasizes whole, nutrient-dense foods, including vegetables, fruits, lean proteins, and healthy fats.
2. The Galveston Diet aims to provide a balanced intake of macronutrients, including proteins, fats, and carbohydrates.
3. The diet encourages the consumption of anti-inflammatory foods, which may have potential health benefits, especially for those dealing with inflammation-related issues.
4. The diet is specifically designed to address hormonal imbalances that women may experience during perimenopause and menopause, potentially helping with symptoms such as weight gain and mood swings.
5. Emphasizing the consumption of anti-inflammatory foods, the Galveston Diet becomes a shield against chronic inflammation. This not only aids in weight loss but significantly reduces the risk of chronic diseases like heart disease, diabetes, and cancer.
6. The inclusion of intermittent fasting becomes a game-changer, helping women shed unwanted weight by strategically reducing calorie intake. Beyond weight loss, intermittent fasting showcases additional merits such as improved insulin sensitivity, lower blood pressure, and a decrease in overall inflammation.
7. One of the Galveston diet's strengths lies in its adaptability. While providing guidelines on what and when to eat, the program remains highly customizable to fit each woman's unique needs and preferences. This flexibility ensures that the diet seamlessly integrates into individual lifestyles.
8. The Galveston Diet liberates followers from the tedious task of counting calories. Instead, it focuses on fostering healthy eating and exercise habits, setting the stage for long-term success rather than relying on restrictive crash diets.

9. Introducing the 16:8 diet, the Galveston Diet helps prevent late-night eating or snacking. However, it encourages mindful eating during the feeding window to prevent overeating and maintain balance.

10. The diet is versatile, accommodating plant-based eaters by allowing adjustments to make it vegetarian- or vegan-friendly. While not eliminating animal-based foods, it provides room for diverse dietary preferences.

Beyond the diet itself, the Galveston approach extends to comprehensive support and guidance. Recognizing the unique challenges faced by women during perimenopause and menopause, the program fills a crucial knowledge gap often overlooked by conventional medical advice.

Measurement Conversion

Dry Measurements Chart

Measurement	Equivalent
1 cup	240 ml
1 tablespoon	15 ml
1 teaspoon	5 ml
1 ounce	28.35 grams
1 pound	453.59 grams

Volume: ml in Teaspoons

Milliliters (ml)	Teaspoons (tsp)
5 mL	1 teaspoon
15 mL	3 teaspoons
30 mL	6 teaspoons
60 mL	12 teaspoons
120 mL	24 teaspoons

Oven Temperatures

Measurement	Equivalent
1 cup	240 ml
1 tablespoon	15 ml
1 teaspoon	5 ml

Baking in Grams

Measurement	Equivalent
1 cup	120 grams
1 tablespoon	15 grams
1 teaspoon	5 grams

1 ounce	28.35 grams
1 pound	453.59 grams

1 ounce	28.35 grams
1 pound	453.59 grams

Liquid Measurement Conversion Chart

Measurement	Equivalent
1 cup	240 ml
1 fluid ounce	29.57 ml
1 pint	473.18 ml
1 quart	946.35 ml
1 gallon	3,785.41 ml

Weight

Pounds (lbs)	Kilograms (kg)
1 pound	0.4536 kg
2 pounds	0.9072 kg
5 pounds	2.268 kg
10 pounds	4.536 kg
20 pounds	9.072 kg

WHOLE GRAINS MEALS

1. Brown Rice and Black Bean Bowl

2. Farro and Roasted Vegetable Stir-Fry

3. Whole Wheat Pasta Primavera

4. Barley and Mushroom Risotto

5. Buckwheat Groats and Chickpea Salad

6. Millet and Spinach Stuffed Peppers

7. Sorghum Buddha Bowl

8. Freekeh Pilaf with Pistachios

9. Wild Rice and Pecan Salad

10. Amaranth Porridge with Berries

11. Sweet Potato and Black Bean Chili

12. Kamut Grain and Vegetable Curry

13. Oatmeal Breakfast Bowl with Nut Butter

Brown Rice and Black Bean Bowl

INGREDIENTS:

1 cup brown rice (uncooked), 1 can (15 ounces) black beans (drained and rinsed), 1 cup corn kernels (fresh or frozen), 1 red bell pepper (diced), 1 avocado (sliced), ¼ cup chopped fresh cilantro, 1 lime (juiced), Salt and pepper to taste.

Servings: 4

Cooking Time: 30 minutes

DIRECTIONS:

a) Cook 1 cup of brown rice in boiling water for 45 minutes or until tender.
b) In a large skillet over medium heat, combine black beans, corn, and red bell pepper. Cook until heated through.
c) In a serving bowl, layer cooked brown rice with the black bean mixture.
d) Top with avocado slices and chopped cilantro.
e) Drizzle lime juice over the bowl and season with salt and pepper to taste.
f) Toss everything gently to combine.

NUTRITION PER SERVING:

Calories: 350, Protein: 10g, Carbohydrates: 60g, Dietary Fiber: 12g, Fat: 8g, Saturated Fat: 1g, Cholesterol: 0mg, Sodium: 350mg

Farro and Roasted Vegetable Stir-Fry

INGREDIENTS:

1 cup farro (uncooked), 2 cups broccoli florets, 1 red bell pepper (sliced), 1 yellow bell pepper (sliced), 1 zucchini (sliced), 1 carrot (julienned) 3 tablespoons soy sauce, 2 tablespoons sesame oil, 1 tablespoon rice vinegar, 1 tablespoon honey or maple syrup, 2 cloves garlic (minced), 1 teaspoon grated ginger, Sesame seeds for garnish (optional), Green onions (chopped), for garnish (optional)

Servings: 4

Cooking Time: 40 minutes

DIRECTIONS:

a) Cook farro in boiling water until tender, about 25 minutes. Preheat the oven to 400°F (200°C).
b) On a baking sheet, toss broccoli, red bell pepper, yellow bell pepper, zucchini, and carrot with 1 tablespoon of sesame oil. Roast in the oven for 20-25 minutes or until vegetables are tender and slightly caramelized.
c) In a small bowl, whisk together soy sauce, remaining sesame oil, rice vinegar, honey, or maple syrup (minced) garlic, and grated ginger to make the sauce.
d) In a large skillet or wok over medium heat, combine cooked farro, roasted vegetables, and the sauce. Stir-fry for 5-7 minutes until everything is well-coated and heated through.
e) Garnish with sesame seeds and chopped green onions if desired.

NUTRITION PER SERVING: Calories: 380, Protein: 8g, Carbohydrates: 65g, Dietary Fiber: 10g, Fat: 12g, Saturated Fat: 1.5g, Cholesterol: 0mg, Sodium: 700mg

Whole Wheat Pasta Primavera

INGREDIENTS:

8 ounces whole wheat pasta, 2 tablespoons olive oil, 3 cloves garlic (minced), 1 red bell pepper (thinly sliced), 1 yellow bell pepper (thinly sliced), 1 zucchini (thinly sliced), 1 carrot (julienned), 1 cup cherry tomatoes (halved), 1 cup broccoli florets, ½ cup peas (fresh or frozen), ¼ cup chopped fresh basil, Salt and pepper to taste (grated) Parmesan cheese for serving (optional)

Servings: 4

Cooking Time: 20 minutes

DIRECTIONS:

a) Cook whole wheat pasta in boiling water until al dente. Drain and set aside.
b) In a large skillet, heat olive oil over medium heat. Add minced garlic and sauté for 2 minutes until fragrant.
c) Add sliced red and yellow bell peppers, zucchini, carrot, cherry tomatoes, broccoli, and peas to the skillet. Stir-fry for about 5-7 minutes or until the vegetables are tender-crisp.
d) Toss in the cooked whole wheat pasta and chopped basil. Mix well to combine.
e) Season with salt and pepper to taste.
f) Serve hot, optionally garnished with grated Parmesan cheese.

NUTRITION PER SERVING:

Calories: 320, Protein: 12g, Carbohydrates: 55g, Dietary Fiber: 10g, Fat: 8g, Saturated Fat: 1g, Cholesterol: 0mg, Sodium: 80mg.

Barley and Mushroom Risotto

INGREDIENTS:

1 cup pearl barley, 4 cups vegetable broth, 2 tablespoons olive oil, 1 onion (fincly chopped), 2 cloves garlic (minced), 8 ounces mushrooms (sliced) (such as cremini or button mushrooms), ½ cup dry white wine (optional), ½ cup grated Parmesan cheese, Salt and pepper to taste, Fresh parsley (chopped)

Servings: 4

Cooking Time: 40 minutes

DIRECTIONS:

a) Simmer vegetable broth in a saucepan over low heat.
b) Sauté chopped onion in olive oil until translucent in a large skillet.
c) Cook minced garlic and sliced mushrooms until browned and tender.
d) Toast pearl barley in the skillet for 1-2 minutes.
e) If using, add and evaporate white wine.
f) Gradually add warm vegetable broth, stirring until absorbed before each addition.
g) Continue until barley is tender and creamy (about 30-35 minutes).
h) Stir in Parmesan cheese, and season with salt and pepper. Garnish with fresh parsley before serving.

NUTRITION PER SERVING:

Calories: 320, Protein: 10g, Carbohydrates: 50g, Dietary Fiber: 10g, Fat: 8g, Saturated Fat: 2g, Cholesterol: 10mg, Sodium: 800mg

Buckwheat Groats and Chickpea Salad

INGREDIENTS:

1 cup buckwheat groats, 1 can (15 ounces) chickpeas (drained and rinsed), 1 cup cherry tomatoes (halved), 1 cucumber (diced), ¼ cup red onion (finely chopped), ¼ cup fresh parsley (chopped), Salt and pepper to taste.

Servings: 4

Cooking Time: 20 minutes

DIRECTIONS:

a) Rinse the buckwheat groats under cold water. In a medium saucepan, bring 2 cups of water to a boil. Add the buckwheat groats, reduce heat to low, cover, and simmer for 15 minutes or until tender. Drain any excess water.

b) In a large mixing bowl, combine the cooked buckwheat groats, chickpeas, cherry tomatoes, cucumber, red onion, and fresh parsley.

c) Season with salt and pepper to taste. Toss the salad gently to combine all the ingredients evenly.

d) Serve immediately or refrigerate for a couple of hours to let the flavors meld.

NUTRITION PER SERVING:

Calories: 250, Protein: 10g, Carbohydrates: 45g, Dietary Fiber: 8g, Fat: 3g, Saturated Fat: 0g, Cholesterol: 0mg, Sodium: 300mg

Millet and Spinach Stuffed Peppers

INGREDIENTS:

1 cup millet (cooked), 4 large bell peppers (halved) and seeds removed, 2 cups fresh spinach (chopped), 1 can (15 ounces) black beans (drained and rinsed), 1 cup corn kernels (fresh or frozen), 1 cup cherry tomatoes (diced), ½ cup red onion (finely chopped), 2 cloves garlic (minced), 1 teaspoon cumin, 1 teaspoon paprika, Salt and pepper to taste, 1 cup shredded cheese (optional, for topping)

Servings: 8

Cooking Time: 30 minutes

DIRECTIONS:

a) Preheat the oven to 375°F (190°C).

b) In a large mixing bowl, combine the cooked millet (chopped) spinach, black beans, corn, cherry tomatoes, red onion (minced) garlic, cumin, paprika, salt, and pepper.

c) Mix the ingredients thoroughly until well combined.

d) Stuff each bell pepper half with the millet and spinach mixture, pressing it down gently.

e) Place the stuffed peppers in a baking dish. If desired, top each stuffed pepper with a sprinkle of shredded cheese.

f) Bake in the preheated oven for 20-25 minutes or until the peppers are tender.

g) Remove from the oven and let them cool for a few minutes before serving.

NUTRITION PER SERVING: Calories: 220, Protein: 9g, Carbohydrates: 42g, Dietary Fiber: 8g, Fat: 2g, Saturated Fat: 1g, Cholesterol: 5mg, Sodium: 300mg

Sorghum Buddha Bowl

INGREDIENTS:

1 cup sorghum (cooked), 2 cups mixed greens (kale, spinach, arugula, etc.), 1 cup roasted sweet potatoes (diced), 1 cup cherry tomatoes (halved), ½ cup cucumber (sliced), ½ cup shredded carrots, ¼ cup red cabbage (thinly sliced), ¼ cup avocado (sliced), ¼ cup almonds (chopped), 2 tablespoons tahini dressing

Servings: 2

Cooking Time: 30 minutes

DIRECTIONS:

a) Cook sorghum in boiling water for approximately 50 minutes or until tender. Allow it to cool slightly.
b) In two bowls, arrange the mixed greens, roasted sweet potatoes, cherry tomatoes, cucumber (shredded) carrots, red cabbage, avocado, and cooked sorghum.
c) Drizzle each bowl with tahini dressing.
d) Sprinkle chopped almonds over the top for added crunch.
e) Toss the ingredients gently or leave them arranged for a visually appealing Buddha bowl..

NUTRITION PER SERVING:

Calories: 500, Protein: 12g, Carbohydrates: 70g, Dietary Fiber: 15g, Fat: 20g, Saturated Fat: 2g, Cholesterol: 0mg, Sodium: 150mg

Freekeh Pilaf with Pistachios

INGREDIENTS:

1 cup freekeh (rinsed and drained), 2 cups vegetable broth, ½ cup shelled pistachios (chopped), ¼ cup dried cranberries, ¼ cup red onion (finely chopped), ¼ cup fresh mint (chopped), 2 tablespoons olive oil, Salt and pepper to taste

Servings: 4

Cooking Time: 25 minutes

DIRECTIONS:

a) In a medium saucepan, bring the vegetable broth to a boil. Add the rinsed freekeh, reduce heat to low, cover, and simmer for 20 minutes or until the freekeh is tender and the liquid is absorbed. Fluff with a fork.

b) In a large mixing bowl, combine the cooked freekeh (chopped) pistachios, dried cranberries, red onion, and fresh mint.

c) Drizzle olive oil over the mixture and toss gently to combine. Season with salt and pepper to taste.

d) Serve the Freekeh Pilaf warm as a side dish or a light main course.

NUTRITION PER SERVING:

Calories: 300, Protein: 8g, Carbohydrates: 40g, Dietary Fiber: 6g, Fat: 14g, Saturated Fat: 2g, Cholesterol: 0mg, Sodium: 500mg

Wild Rice and Pecan Salad

INGREDIENTS:

1 cup wild rice (cooked), ½ cup pecans (toasted and chopped), 1 cup mixed bell peppers (diced), ½ cup dried cranberries, ¼ cup red onion (finely chopped), ¼ cup fresh parsley (chopped), 2 tablespoons olive oil, 2 tablespoons balsamic vinegar, Salt and pepper to taste

Servings: 4

Cooking Time: 30 minutes

DIRECTIONS:

a) Cook the wild rice in boiling water for 45-55 minutes or until tender. Once cooked, allow it to cool.
b) In a dry skillet over medium heat, toast the pecans for 3-5 minutes, stirring frequently, until fragrant. Remove from heat and let them cool before chopping.
c) In a large mixing bowl, combine the cooked wild rice (chopped) pecans (diced) bell peppers, dried cranberries, red onion, and fresh parsley.
d) In a small bowl, whisk together the olive oil and balsamic vinegar. Pour the dressing over the salad and toss gently to combine.
e) Season with salt and pepper to taste.
f) Serve the Wild Rice and Pecan Salad at room temperature or chilled.

NUTRITION PER SERVING:

Calories: 300, Protein: 6g, Carbohydrates: 40g, Dietary Fiber: 5g, Fat: 14g, Saturated Fat: 1.5g, Cholesterol: 0mg, Sodium: 100mg

Amaranth Porridge with Berries

INGREDIENTS:

½ cup amaranth, 2 cups unsweetened almond milk, 1 cup mixed berries (strawberries, blueberries, raspberries), 2 tablespoons maple syrup or honey, ¼ cup chopped nuts (almonds, walnuts, or pecans), 1 teaspoon vanilla extract, Pinch of cinnamon, Pinch of salt

Servings: 2

Cooking Time: 25 minutes

DIRECTIONS:

a) Rinse the amaranth under cold water.
b) In a medium saucepan, combine the rinsed amaranth and almond milk. Bring to a boil, then reduce heat to low, cover, and simmer for 20-25 minutes or until the amaranth is tender and the liquid is absorbed.
c) Stir in the vanilla extract, cinnamon, and a pinch of salt.
d) Divide the amaranth porridge into serving bowls.
e) Top each bowl with mixed berries (chopped) and nuts, and drizzle with maple syrup or honey.

NUTRITION PER SERVING:

Calories: 300, Protein: 8g, Carbohydrates: 50g, Dietary Fiber: 8g, Fat: 10g, Saturated Fat: 1g, Cholesterol: 0mg, Sodium: 150mg

Sweet Potato and Black Bean Chili

INGREDIENTS:

2 medium sweet potatoes (peeled and diced), 1 can (15 ounces) black beans (drained and rinsed), 1 can (14 ounces) diced tomatoes (undrained), 1 cup corn kernels (fresh or frozen), 1 onion (diced), 2 cloves garlic (minced), 1 red bell pepper (diced), 1 green bell pepper (diced), 1 tablespoon chili powder, 1 teaspoon cumin, 1 teaspoon smoked paprika, ½ teaspoon cinnamon, Salt and pepper to taste, 4 cups vegetable broth, 2 tablespoons olive oil

Servings: 6

Cooking Time: 30 minutes

DIRECTIONS:

a) In a large pot, heat olive oil over medium heat. Add diced onions and garlic, and sauté until softened.

b) Add sweet potatoes, and red and green bell peppers, and cook for 5 minutes.

c) Stir in chili powder, cumin, smoked paprika, cinnamon, salt, and pepper. Cook for an additional 2 minutes to toast the spices.

d) Add black beans (diced) tomatoes, corn, and vegetable broth to the pot. Bring to a boil, then reduce heat and simmer for 20-25 minutes or until sweet potatoes are tender.

e) Adjust seasoning to taste.

f)   Serve the Sweet Potato and Black Bean Chili hot, garnished with your favorite toppings.

NUTRITION PER SERVING: Calories: 300, Protein: 8g, Carbohydrates: 55g, Dietary Fiber: 12g, Fat: 7g, Saturated Fat: 1g, Cholesterol: 0mg, Sodium: 800mg

Kamut Grain and Vegetable Curry

INGREDIENTS:

1 cup Kamut grain (soaked and drained), 2 cups mixed vegetables (carrots, broccoli, bell peppers, peas), 1 can (14 ounces) chickpeas (drained and rinsed), 1 onion (finely chopped), 3 cloves garlic (minced), 1 tablespoon curry powder, 1 teaspoon ground turmeric, 1 teaspoon ground cumin, 1 teaspoon paprika, 1 can (14 ounces) coconut milk, 1 cup vegetable broth, 2 tablespoons olive oil, Salt and pepper to taste, Fresh cilantro for garnish

Servings: 4

Cooking Time: 40 minutes

DIRECTIONS:

a) In a large pot, heat olive oil over medium heat. Add chopped onions and sauté until translucent.

b) Add minced garlic, curry powder, ground turmeric, ground cumin, and paprika. Stir well and cook for 2-3 minutes to release the flavors.

c) Add soaked and drained Kamut grain to the pot. Stir to coat the grains with the spice mixture.

d) Pour in the coconut milk and vegetable broth. Bring to a boil, then reduce heat to low, cover, and simmer for 25-30 minutes or until Kamut is tender.

e) Add mixed vegetables and chickpeas to the pot. Cook for an additional 10 minutes or until the vegetables are tender.

f) Season the curry with salt and pepper to taste.

g) Serve the Kamut Grain and Vegetable Curry hot, garnished with fresh cilantro.

NUTRITION PER SERVING: Calories: 400, Protein: 12g, Carbohydrates: 50g, Dietary Fiber: 10g, Fat: 18g, Saturated Fat: 10g, Cholesterol: 0mg, Sodium: 600mg

Oatmeal Breakfast Bowl with Nut Butter

INGREDIENTS:

1 cup old-fashioned oats, 2 cups unsweetened almond milk, 2 tablespoons almond butter or any nut butter of choice, 1 banana (sliced), ¼ cup berries, 1 tablespoon chia seeds, 1 tablespoon honey or maple syrup (optional, for sweetness), A pinch of salt.

Servings: 2

Cooking Time: 10 minutes

DIRECTIONS:

a) In a saucepan, combine the old-fashioned oats, almond milk, and a pinch of salt.
b) Bring to a simmer over medium heat.
c) Reduce heat to low and cook the oats, stirring occasionally, for about 5-7 minutes or until they reach your desired consistency.
d) Remove the saucepan from heat and stir in almond butter until well combined.
e) Divide the oatmeal into two bowls.
f) Top each bowl with sliced banana, berries, and chia seeds.
g) If desired, drizzle with honey or maple syrup for added sweetness.

NUTRITION PER SERVING:

Calories: 400, Protein: 10g, Carbohydrates: 60g, Dietary Fiber: 10g, Fat: 15g, Saturated Fat: 1.5g, Cholesterol: 0mg, Sodium: 200mg

LEGUMES MEALS

14. Chickpea and Vegetable Stir-Fry

15. Black Bean and Avocado Salad

16. Edamame and Quinoa Bowl

17. Hummus and Veggie Wrap

18. Kidney Bean and Turkey Chili

19. Cannellini Bean and Tuna Salad

20. Chana Masala with Brown Rice

21. Mung Bean Salad with Cilantro-Lime Dressing

22. Black-Eyed Pea and Collard Green Stew

23. White Bean and Roasted Vegetable Wrap

24. Adzuki Bean and Sweet Potato Curry

25. Lima Bean and Tomato Salad

Chickpea and Vegetable Stir-Fry

INGREDIENTS:

1 can (15 ounces) chickpeas (drained and rinsed), 2 cups mixed vegetables (broccoli, bell peppers, snap peas, carrots) (chopped), 1 cup snow peas, ends trimmed, ½ cup red onion (sliced), 3 cloves garlic (minced), 1 tablespoon ginger (grated), 3 tablespoons low-sodium soy sauce, 1 tablespoon sesame oil, 1 tablespoon olive oil, 1 tablespoon rice vinegar, 1 tablespoon honey or maple syrup (optional, for sweetness), Sesame seeds for garnish, Green onions (sliced), for garnish (cooked) brown rice or quinoa for serving

Servings: 4

Cooking Time: 15

DIRECTIONS:

a) In a large wok or skillet, heat olive oil over medium-high heat.
b) Add sliced red onion (minced) garlic, and grated ginger. Stir-fry for 1-2 minutes until fragrant.
c) Add the mixed vegetables, snow peas, and chickpeas to the wok. Stir-fry for 5-7 minutes or until the vegetables are tender-crisp.
d) In a small bowl, whisk together soy sauce, sesame oil, rice vinegar, and honey (if using).
e) Pour the sauce over the vegetables and chickpeas. Toss everything to coat evenly and cook for an additional 2-3 minutes.
f) Remove from heat. Serve the Chickpea and Vegetable Stir-Fry over cooked brown rice or quinoa.
g) Garnish with sesame seeds and sliced green onions.

NUTRITION PER SERVING: Calories: 350, Protein: 10g, Carbohydrates: 50g, Dietary Fiber: 10g, Fat: 12g, Saturated Fat: 1.5g, Cholesterol: 0mg, Sodium: 600mg

Black Bean and Avocado Salad

INGREDIENTS:

2 cans (15 ounces each) black beans (drained and rinsed), 2 avocados (diced), 1 cup corn kernels (fresh or frozen), 1 cup cherry tomatoes (halved), ¼ cup red onion (finely chopped), ¼ cup fresh cilantro (chopped), 2 tablespoons olive oil, 1 tablespoon lime juice, 1 teaspoon cumin, Salt and pepper to taste

Servings: 4

Preparation Time: 15 minutes

DIRECTIONS:

a) In a large mixing bowl, combine the black beans (diced) avocados, corn, cherry tomatoes, red onion, and chopped cilantro.
b) In a small bowl, whisk together olive oil, lime juice, cumin, salt, and pepper to create the dressing.
c) Pour the dressing over the salad ingredients.
d) Gently toss the salad until all ingredients are evenly coated with the dressing.
e) Serve the Black Bean and Avocado Salad immediately or refrigerate for a short time before serving.

NUTRITION PER SERVING:

Calories: 350, Protein: 12g, Carbohydrates: 45g, Dietary Fiber: 14g, Fat: 15g, Saturated Fat: 2g, Cholesterol: 0mg, Sodium: 600mg

Edamame and Quinoa Bowl

INGREDIENTS:

1 cup quinoa (rinsed), 2 cups edamame (shelled), 1 red bell pepper (diced), 1 cucumber (sliced), ¼ cup red onion (finely chopped), ¼ cup fresh cilantro (chopped), 2 tablespoons soy sauce, 1 tablespoon rice vinegar, 1 tablespoon sesame oil, 1 tablespoon honey or maple syrup (optional, for sweetness), Sesame seeds for garnish

Servings: 4

Cooking Time: 20 minutes

DIRECTIONS:

a) Cook quinoa in boiling water for about 15 minutes or until the grains are translucent. Once cooked, let it cool.

b) In a large mixing bowl, combine cooked quinoa (shelled) edamame (diced) red bell pepper (sliced) cucumber (chopped) red onion, and cilantro.

c) In a small bowl, whisk together soy sauce, rice vinegar, sesame oil, and honey (if using).

d) Pour the dressing over the quinoa and edamame mixture. Toss everything to coat evenly.

e) Serve the Edamame and Quinoa Bowl garnished with sesame seeds.

NUTRITION PER SERVING:

Calories: 350, Protein: 15g, Carbohydrates: 45g, Dietary Fiber: 8g, Fat: 12g, Saturated Fat: 1.5g, Cholesterol: 0mg, Sodium: 600mg

Hummus and Veggie Wrap

INGREDIENTS:

1 whole-grain or sprouted-grain wrap, ½ cup hummus (store-bought or homemade), 1 cup mixed veggies (bell peppers, cucumber, cherry tomatoes (shredded) carrots), ¼ cup red onion (thinly sliced), ¼ cup fresh spinach or lettuce leaves, 1 tablespoon olive oil, 1 tablespoon lemon juice, Salt and pepper to taste

Servings: 1

Preparation Time: 10 minutes

DIRECTIONS:

a) Lay the wrap on a flat surface.
b) Spread a generous layer of hummus evenly over the wrap, leaving a border around the edges.
c) In the center of the wrap, arrange the mixed veggies, red onion, and fresh spinach or lettuce leaves.
d) Drizzle olive oil and lemon juice over the veggies. Sprinkle with salt and pepper to taste.
e) Carefully fold in the sides of the wrap and then roll it up tightly from the bottom.
f) Slice the wrap in half diagonally, if desired, and serve.

NUTRITION PER SERVING:

Calories: 400, Protein: 12g, Carbohydrates: 50g, Dietary Fiber: 10g, Fat: 18g, Saturated Fat: 2g, Cholesterol: 0mg, Sodium: 600mg

Kidney Bean and Turkey Chili

INGREDIENTS:

1 pound ground turkey, 2 cans (15 ounces each) kidney beans (drained and rinsed), 1 can (14 ounces) diced tomatoes (undrained), 1 cup corn kernels (fresh or frozen), 1 onion (diced), 2 cloves garlic (minced), 1 red bell pepper (diced), 1 green bell pepper (diced), 2 tablespoons chili powder, 1 teaspoon cumin, 1 teaspoon paprika, ½ teaspoon cinnamon, Salt and pepper to taste, 4 cups low-sodium chicken or vegetable broth, 2 tablespoons olive oil

Servings: 6

Cooking Time: 40 minutes

DIRECTIONS:

a) In a large pot, heat olive oil over medium heat. Add diced onions and minced garlic, and sauté until softened.

b) Add ground turkey to the pot. Cook until browned, breaking it apart with a spoon.

c) Stir in chili powder, cumin, paprika, cinnamon, salt, and pepper. Cook for an additional 2 minutes to enhance the flavors.

d) Add kidney beans (diced) tomatoes, corn (diced) red and green bell peppers, and chicken or vegetable broth to the pot. Bring to a boil, then reduce heat and simmer for 30 minutes.

e) Adjust seasoning to taste.

f) Serve the Kidney Bean and Turkey Chili hot, garnished with your favorite toppings.

NUTRITION PER SERVING: Calories: 350, Protein: 20g, Carbohydrates: 40g, Dietary Fiber: 10g, Fat: 12g, Saturated Fat: 2.5g, Cholesterol: 40mg, Sodium: 700mg

Cannellini Bean and Tuna Salad

INGREDIENTS:

2 cans (15 ounces each) cannellini beans (drained and rinsed), 2 cans (5 ounces each) tuna in water (drained), 1 cup cherry tomatoes (halved), ¼ cup red onion (finely chopped), ¼ cup fresh parsley (chopped), 2 tablespoons olive oil, 1 tablespoon red wine vinegar, 1 teaspoon Dijon mustard, Salt and pepper to taste

Servings: 4

Preparation Time: 15 minutes

DIRECTIONS:

a) In a large mixing bowl, combine the cannellini beans (drained) tuna, cherry tomatoes (chopped) red onion, and fresh parsley.

b) In a small bowl, whisk together olive oil, red wine vinegar, Dijon mustard, salt, and pepper to create the dressing.

c) Pour the dressing over the salad ingredients.

d) Gently toss the Cannellini Bean and Tuna Salad until all ingredients are evenly coated with the dressing.

e) Serve the salad immediately or refrigerate for a short time before serving.

NUTRITION PER SERVING: Calories: 350, Protein: 25g, Carbohydrates: 35g, Dietary Fiber: 10g, Fat: 15g, Saturated Fat: 2.5g, Cholesterol: 30mg, Sodium: 600mg

Chana Masala with Brown Rice

INGREDIENTS:

2 cans (15 ounces each) chickpeas (drained and rinsed), 1 onion (finely chopped), 3 tomatoes (diced), 2 cloves garlic (minced), 1 tablespoon ginger (grated), 1 can (14 ounces) tomato sauce, ¼ cup cilantro (chopped) (for garnish), ¼ cup plain Greek yogurt (optional, for serving), 2 tablespoons olive oil, 1 tablespoon garam masala, 1 teaspoon ground cumin, 1 teaspoon ground coriander, 1 teaspoon turmeric, ½ teaspoon cayenne pepper (adjust to taste), Salt and pepper to taste, 4 cups cooked brown rice

Servings: 4

Cooking Time: 30 minutes

DIRECTIONS:

a) In a large skillet or pot, heat olive oil over medium heat. Add chopped onions and sauté until translucent.

b) Add minced garlic and grated ginger. Sauté for an additional 1-2 minutes until fragrant.

c) Stir in garam masala, ground cumin, ground coriander, turmeric, cayenne pepper, salt, and pepper. Cook for 2-3 minutes to toast the spices.

d) Add diced tomatoes and cook until they soften.

e) Pour in the tomato sauce and bring the mixture to a simmer.

f) Add drained chickpeas and cook for 15-20 minutes, allowing the flavors to meld and the chickpeas to absorb the spices.

g) Adjust the seasoning to taste.

h) Serve the Chana Masala over cooked brown rice, garnished with chopped cilantro.

i) Optionally, top with a dollop of plain Greek yogurt before serving.

NUTRITION PER SERVING: Calories: 400, Protein: 15g, Carbohydrates: 65g, Dietary Fiber: 12g, Fat: 10g, Saturated Fat: 1.5g, Cholesterol: 0mg, Sodium: 800mg

Mung Bean Salad with Cilantro-Lime Dressing

INGREDIENTS:

1 cup mung beans (soaked and cooked), 1 cup cucumber (diced), 1 cup cherry tomatoes (halved), ¼ cup red onion (finely chopped), ¼ cup fresh cilantro (chopped), 2 tablespoons olive oil, 1 tablespoon lemon juice, Salt and pepper to taste

Servings: 4

Preparation Time: 15 minutes

DIRECTIONS:

a) Cook the soaked mung beans according to package instructions. Once cooked, let them cool.
b) In a large mixing bowl, combine the cooked mung beans (diced) cucumber (halved) cherry tomatoes (chopped) red onion, and fresh cilantro.
c) In a small bowl, whisk together olive oil, lemon juice, salt, and pepper to create the dressing.
d) Pour the dressing over the salad ingredients.
e) Gently toss the Mung Bean Salad until all ingredients are evenly coated with the dressing.
f) Serve the salad immediately or refrigerate for a short time before serving.

NUTRITION PER SERVING: Calories: 200, Protein: 10g, Carbohydrates: 30g, Dietary Fiber: 8g, Fat: 6g, Saturated Fat: 1g, Cholesterol: 0mg, Sodium: 200mg

Black-Eyed Pea and Collard Green Stew

INGREDIENTS:

1 cup dried black-eyed peas (soaked overnight), 1 bunch collard greens (stems removed and leaves chopped), 1 onion (finely chopped), 3 cloves garlic (minced), 1 carrot (diced), 1 celery stalk (chopped), 1 can (14 ounces) diced tomatoes, 4 cups vegetable broth, 1 teaspoon smoked paprika, ½ teaspoon cayenne pepper, Salt and pepper to taste, 2 tablespoons olive oil

Servings: 4

Preparation Time: 15 minutes (plus soaking time for black-eyed peas)

DIRECTIONS:

a) In a large pot, heat olive oil over medium heat. Add chopped onions and sauté until translucent.
b) Add minced garlic (diced) carrots, and chopped celery. Cook until the vegetables are softened.
c) Drain the soaked black-eyed peas and add them to the pot.
d) Pour in the diced tomatoes with their juice, smoked paprika, cayenne pepper, salt, and pepper. Stir to combine. Add the vegetable broth and bring the stew to a boil. Reduce the heat to low, cover, and simmer for about 30-40 minutes or until the black-eyed peas are tender. Stir in the chopped collard greens and cook for an additional 10-15 minutes until the greens are wilted and cooked through. Serve hot.

NUTRITION PER SERVING:

Calories: 250, Protein: 10g, Carbohydrates: 40g, Dietary Fiber: 8g, Fat: 6g, Sodium: 800mg

White Bean and Roasted Vegetable Wrap

INGREDIENTS:

1 can (15 ounces) white beans (drained and rinsed), 1 zucchini (sliced), 1 red bell pepper (sliced), 1 yellow bell pepper (sliced), 1 red onion (thinly sliced), 2 tablespoons olive oil, 1 teaspoon dried oregano, Salt and pepper to taste, 4 whole wheat wraps, 1 cup baby spinach leaves, ½ cup feta cheese (crumbled), Greek yogurt or tzatziki sauce for serving

Servings: 4

Preparation Time: 15 minutes

DIRECTIONS:

a) Preheat the oven to 400°F (200°C).
b) In a large bowl, combine the sliced zucchini, red and yellow bell peppers, and red onion. Drizzle with olive oil, and sprinkle with dried oregano, salt, and pepper. Toss to coat the vegetables evenly.
c) Spread the vegetables on a baking sheet in a single layer. Roast in the preheated oven for about 20-25 minutes or until the vegetables are tender and slightly caramelized. While the vegetables are roasting, prepare the white beans. Mash them slightly with a fork in a bowl. Warm the whole wheat wraps in a dry skillet or microwave. Assemble the wraps by spreading a layer of mashed white beans on each wrap. Top with roasted vegetables, a handful of baby spinach, and crumbled feta cheese. Drizzle with Greek yogurt or tzatziki. Fold in the sides and roll up the wraps tightly.

NUTRITION PER SERVING:

Calories: 380, Protein: 14g, Carbohydrates: 52g, Dietary Fiber: 10g, Fat: 14g, Sodium: 580mg

Adzuki Bean and Sweet Potato Curry

INGREDIENTS:

1 cup adzuki beans (soaked overnight), 2 sweet potatoes (peeled and diced), 1 onion (finely chopped), 3 cloves garlic (minced), 1 can (14 ounces) coconut milk, 1 can (14 ounces) diced tomatoes, 1 tablespoon curry powder, 1 teaspoon ground cumin, 1 teaspoon ground coriander, ½ teaspoon turmeric, Salt and pepper to taste, 2 tablespoons vegetable oil, Fresh cilantro for garnish

Servings: 4

Preparation Time: 15 minutes (plus soaking time for adzuki beans)

DIRECTIONS:

a) In a large pot, heat vegetable oil over medium heat. Add chopped onions and sauté until softened.
b) Add minced garlic, curry powder, ground cumin, ground coriander, and turmeric. Stir for 1-2 minutes until fragrant. Drain the soaked adzuki beans and add them to the pot along with diced sweet potatoes. Stir to coat the beans and sweet potatoes with the spices. Pour in the coconut milk and diced tomatoes (with their juice). Season with salt and pepper. Bring the curry to a boil.
c) Reduce the heat to low, cover, and simmer for about 30-40 minutes or until the adzuki beans are tender and the sweet potatoes are cooked through. Adjust the seasoning if needed.
d) Serve the curry over rice or your preferred grain. Garnish with fresh cilantro before serving.

NUTRITION PER SERVING:

Calories: 380, Protein: 12g, Carbohydrates: 52g, Dietary Fiber: 11g, Fat: 15g, Sodium: 520mg

Lima Bean and Tomato Salad

INGREDIENTS:

2 cups cooked lima beans, 1 cup cherry tomatoes (halved), ½ red onion (finely chopped), ¼ cup fresh parsley (chopped), 2 tablespoons olive oil, 1 tablespoon red wine vinegar, 1 teaspoon Dijon mustard, Salt and pepper to taste

Servings: 4

Preparation Time: 15 minutes (assuming lima beans are pre-cooked)

DIRECTIONS:

a) In a large bowl, combine the cooked lima beans, cherry tomatoes (chopped) red onion, and fresh parsley.
b) In a small bowl, whisk together the olive oil, red wine vinegar, Dijon mustard, salt, and pepper to create the dressing.
c) Pour the dressing over the lima bean mixture and toss gently to coat all the ingredients evenly.
d) Allow the salad to marinate for at least 15 minutes before serving to enhance the flavors.
e) Adjust seasoning if needed and serve at room temperature or chilled.

NUTRITION PER SERVING:

Calories: 180, Protein: 7g, Carbohydrates: 25g, Dietary Fiber: 7g, Fat: 7g, Sodium: 120mg

VEGETABLES & SALADS

26. Mediterranean Chickpea Salad

27. Kale and Berry Salad with Almonds

28. Roasted Brussels Sprouts and Butternut Squash

29. Cucumber and Tomato Greek Salad

30. Spinach and Strawberry Salad

31. Broccoli and Walnut Quinoa Salad

32. Avocado and Tomato Caprese Salad

33. Sweet Potato and Kale Hash

34. Arugula and Pomegranate Salad

35. Roasted Vegetable Frittata

Mediterranean Chickpea Salad

INGREDIENTS:

2 cans (15 ounces each) chickpeas (drained and rinsed), 1 cucumber (diced), 1 cup cherry tomatoes (halved), ½ red onion (finely chopped), ½ cup Kalamata olives (sliced), ½ cup feta cheese (crumbled), ¼ cup fresh parsley (chopped), ¼ cup fresh mint (chopped), ¼ cup extra virgin olive oil, 2 tablespoons red wine vinegar, 1 teaspoon dried oregano, Salt and pepper to taste

Servings: 4

Preparation Time: 15 minutes

DIRECTIONS:

a) In a large bowl, combine the chickpeas (diced) cucumber, cherry tomatoes (chopped) red onion, Kalamata olives (crumbled) feta cheese, fresh parsley, and fresh mint.
b) In a small bowl, whisk together the extra virgin olive oil, red wine vinegar, dried oregano, salt, and pepper to create the dressing.
c) Pour the dressing over the chickpea mixture and toss gently to ensure all ingredients are well coated.
d) Allow the salad to marinate for at least 15 minutes to let the flavors meld.
e) Adjust seasoning if needed and serve chilled.

NUTRITION PER SERVING: Calories: 380, Protein: 14g, Carbohydrates: 38g, Dietary Fiber: 10g, Fat: 20g, Sodium: 680mg

TIPS:

- Add chopped red or yellow bell peppers for additional color and crunch.
- For a heartier meal, serve the salad over a bed of mixed greens or with quinoa.

Kale and Berry Salad with Almonds

INGREDIENTS:

6 cups kale, stems removed and leaves finely chopped, 1 cup mixed berries (strawberries, blueberries, raspberries), ½ cup sliced almonds, ¼ cup feta cheese (crumbled), ¼ cup red onion (thinly sliced), ¼ cup extra virgin olive oil, 2 tablespoons balsamic vinegar, 1 tablespoon honey, Salt and pepper to taste

Servings: 4

Preparation Time: 15 minutes

DIRECTIONS:

a) In a large bowl, combine the finely chopped kale, mixed berries (sliced) almonds (crumbled) feta cheese, and thinly sliced red onion.
b) In a small bowl, whisk together the extra virgin olive oil, balsamic vinegar, honey, salt, and pepper to create the dressing.
c) Pour the dressing over the kale and berry mixture. Toss the salad well to ensure an even coating.
d) Allow the salad to sit for about 5 minutes to allow the kale to soften slightly.
e) Adjust seasoning if needed and serve immediately.

NUTRITION PER SERVING: Calories: 280, Protein: 9g, Carbohydrates: 25g, Dietary Fiber: 5g, Fat: 18g, Sodium: 220mg

TIPS:

● Add grilled chicken or tofu for an extra protein boost.
● Substitute other nuts, such as walnuts or pecans, if you don't have almonds.
● Experiment with different types of berries based on seasonal availability.

Roasted Brussels Sprouts and Butternut Squash

INGREDIENTS:

1 pound Brussels sprouts (trimmed and halved), 1 small butternut squash (peeled, seeded, and diced), 2 tablespoons olive oil, 1 teaspoon dried thyme, 1 teaspoon smoked paprika, Salt and pepper to taste, ¼ cup grated Parmesan cheese (optional)

Servings: 4

Preparation Time: 15 minutes

DIRECTIONS:

a) Preheat the oven to 400°F (200°C).
b) In a large bowl, combine the halved Brussels sprouts and diced butternut squash.
c) Drizzle olive oil over the vegetables and toss to coat evenly.
d) Sprinkle dried thyme, smoked paprika, salt, and pepper over the vegetables. Toss again to distribute the seasonings. Spread the vegetables in a single layer on a baking sheet.
e) Roast in the preheated oven for about 25-30 minutes or until the Brussels sprouts are golden brown and the butternut squash is tender, stirring halfway through.
f) If desired, sprinkle grated Parmesan cheese over the roasted vegetables during the last 5 minutes of baking. Adjust seasoning if needed and serve hot.

NUTRITION PER SERVING: Calories: 180, Protein: 5g, Carbohydrates: 25g, Dietary Fiber: 7g, Fat: 8g, Sodium: 90mg

TIPS:

● Add a drizzle of balsamic glaze or honey for extra sweetness.
● Include chopped garlic or red pepper flakes for added flavor and heat.

Cucumber and Tomato Greek Salad

INGREDIENTS:

2 large cucumbers (diced), 2 cups cherry tomatoes (halved), ½ red onion (thinly sliced), 1 cup Kalamata olives (pitted and sliced), 1 cup feta cheese (crumbled), ¼ cup fresh parsley (chopped), ¼ cup extra virgin olive oil, 2 tablespoons red wine vinegar, 1 teaspoon dried oregano, Salt and pepper to taste

Servings: 4

Preparation Time: 15 minutes

DIRECTIONS:

a) In a large bowl, combine the diced cucumbers (halved) cherry tomatoes (thinly sliced) red onion (sliced) Kalamata olives (crumbled) feta cheese, and chopped fresh parsley.
b) In a small bowl, whisk together the extra virgin olive oil, red wine vinegar, dried oregano, salt, and pepper to create the dressing.
c) Pour the dressing over the cucumber and tomato mixture. Toss the salad gently to ensure all ingredients are well coated.
d) Allow the salad to marinate for at least 15 minutes to let the flavors meld.
e) Adjust seasoning if needed and serve chilled.

NUTRITION PER SERVING: Calories: 320, Protein: 9g, Carbohydrates: 18g, Dietary Fiber: 4g, Fat: 25g, Sodium: 700mg

TIPS:

● Include diced bell peppers for added color and crunch.
● For a more substantial meal, add grilled chicken or shrimp on top of the salad.
● Garnish with a few sprigs of fresh mint for a refreshing twist.
● Serve over a bed of mixed greens or with pita bread on the side.

Spinach and Strawberry Salad

INGREDIENTS:

6 cups fresh baby spinach, 1 pint strawberries (hulled and sliced), ½ cup red onion (thinly sliced), ½ cup feta cheese (crumbled), ¼ cup sliced almonds, ¼ cup balsamic vinaigrette dressing

Servings: 4

Preparation Time: 15 minutes

DIRECTIONS:

a) In a large bowl, combine the fresh baby spinach (sliced) strawberries (thinly sliced) red onion (crumbled) feta cheese, and sliced almonds.
b) Drizzle balsamic vinaigrette dressing over the salad.
c) Toss the salad gently to ensure all ingredients are well coated with the dressing.
d) Adjust seasoning if needed and serve immediately.

NUTRITION PER SERVING:

Calories: 180, Protein: 7g, Carbohydrates: 15g, Dietary Fiber: 5g, Fat: 11g, Sodium: 280mg

TIPS:

- Add grilled chicken or shrimp for a protein boost.
- Substitute other nuts, such as walnuts or pine nuts, if you don't have almonds.
- Drizzle with a touch of honey for extra sweetness.
- For a refreshing twist, add a handful of mint leaves to the salad.

Broccoli and Walnut Quinoa Salad

INGREDIENTS:

1 cup quinoa (rinsed and cooked), 2 cups broccoli florets (blanched), ½ cup walnuts (chopped), ¼ cup red onion (finely chopped), ¼ cup dried cranberries, ¼ cup feta cheese (crumbled), 2 tablespoons extra virgin olive oil, 1 tablespoon balsamic vinegar, Salt and pepper to taste

Servings: 4

Preparation Time: 15 minutes (plus cooking time for quinoa and blanching broccoli)

DIRECTIONS:

a) In a large bowl, combine the cooked quinoa (blanched) broccoli florets (chopped) walnuts (finely chopped) red onion, dried cranberries, and crumbled feta cheese.
b) In a small bowl, whisk together the extra virgin olive oil, balsamic vinegar, salt, and pepper to create the dressing.
c) Pour the dressing over the quinoa and broccoli mixture. Toss the salad gently to ensure all ingredients are well coated.
d) Adjust seasoning if needed and serve chilled.

NUTRITION PER SERVING: Calories: 320, Protein: 9g, Carbohydrates: 38g, Dietary Fiber: 6g, Fat: 16g, Sodium: 180mg

TIPS:

● Add a squeeze of fresh lemon juice for a citrusy kick.
● Include cherry tomatoes or bell peppers for additional color and flavor.
● Toast the walnuts in a dry skillet for a few minutes to enhance their nutty flavor.
● Garnish with fresh herbs like parsley or basil before serving.

Avocado and Tomato Caprese Salad

INGREDIENTS:

3 large tomatoes (sliced), 2 avocados (sliced), 1 ball fresh mozzarella cheese (sliced), Fresh basil leaves, 2 tablespoons balsamic glaze, 2 tablespoons extra virgin olive oil, Salt and pepper to taste

Servings: 4

Preparation Time: 15 minutes

DIRECTIONS:

a) Arrange the sliced tomatoes, avocados, and fresh mozzarella cheese on a serving platter, alternating them.
b) Tuck fresh basil leaves between the slices of tomatoes, avocados, and mozzarella.
c) Drizzle balsamic glaze and extra virgin olive oil over the salad.
d) Sprinkle salt and pepper to taste.
e) Serve immediately, allowing the flavors to meld.

NUTRITION PER SERVING:

Calories: 300, Protein: 9g, Carbohydrates: 14g, Dietary Fiber: 7g, Fat: 25g, Sodium: 320mg

TIPS:

- Use a good quality balsamic glaze for a rich and sweet flavor.
- Add a sprinkle of pine nuts or walnuts for a crunchy element.
- Drizzle with a touch of honey for extra sweetness.
- Serve as a refreshing appetizer or as a side dish to complement grilled chicken or fish.

Sweet Potato and Kale Hash

INGREDIENTS:

2 large sweet potatoes (peeled and diced), 2 cups kale (stems removed and chopped), 1 onion (finely chopped), 2 cloves garlic (minced), 1 teaspoon smoked paprika, ½ teaspoon cayenne pepper (optional), Salt and pepper to taste, 2 tablespoons olive oil

Servings: 4

Preparation Time: 15 minutes

DIRECTIONS:

a) In a large skillet, heat olive oil over medium heat.
b) Add chopped onions and sauté until translucent.
c) Add minced garlic and cook for an additional 1-2 minutes until fragrant.
d) Add diced sweet potatoes to the skillet, spreading them in an even layer. Cook without stirring for a few minutes to allow the edges to brown.
e) Stir in smoked paprika, cayenne pepper (if using), salt, and pepper.
f) Cover the skillet with a lid and cook for about 10-15 minutes, stirring occasionally, until the sweet potatoes are tender. Add chopped kale to the skillet and stir well. Cook for an additional 5 minutes or until the kale is wilted and cooked through.
g) Adjust seasoning if needed and serve hot.

NUTRITION PER SERVING: Calories: 220, Protein: 4g, Carbohydrates: 35g, Dietary Fiber: 6g, Fat: 8g, Sodium: 180mg

TIPS: Top with a fried or poached egg for added protein.

● Sprinkle with crumbled feta or goat cheese before serving.

Arugula and Pomegranate Salad

INGREDIENTS:

6 cups arugula (washed and dried), 1 cup pomegranate arils, ½ cup crumbled goat cheese, ¼ cup walnuts (chopped), 2 tablespoons extra virgin olive oil, 1 tablespoon balsamic vinegar, 1 teaspoon honey, Salt and pepper to taste

Servings: 4

Preparation Time: 15 minutes

DIRECTIONS:

a) In a large bowl, combine the arugula, pomegranate arils (crumbled) goat cheese, and chopped walnuts.
b) In a small bowl, whisk together the extra virgin olive oil, balsamic vinegar, honey, salt, and pepper to create the dressing.
c) Drizzle the dressing over the salad and toss gently to ensure all ingredients are well coated.
d) Adjust seasoning if needed and serve immediately.

NUTRITION PER SERVING:

Calories: 220, Protein: 7g, Carbohydrates: 15g, Dietary Fiber: 3g, Fat: 16g, Sodium: 180mg

TIPS:

● Substitute feta cheese for goat cheese if preferred.
● Add a handful of sliced strawberries or mandarin oranges for extra sweetness.
● Toast the walnuts in a dry skillet for a few minutes to enhance their flavor.
● Drizzle with a balsamic reduction for a more concentrated and sweeter dressing.

Roasted Vegetable Frittata

INGREDIENTS:

1 cup cherry tomatoes (halved), 1 zucchini (diced), 1 bell pepper (diced), 1 cup broccoli florets, 8 large eggs, ¼ cup milk, ½ cup shredded cheddar cheese, 2 tablespoons olive oil, 1 teaspoon dried thyme, Salt and pepper to taste, Fresh herbs for garnish (optional)

Servings: 4-6

Preparation Time: 15 minutes

DIRECTIONS:

a) Preheat the oven to 400°F (200°C).
b) Toss the cherry tomatoes (diced) zucchini (diced) bell pepper, and broccoli florets with olive oil, dried thyme, salt, and pepper. Spread the vegetables in a single layer on a baking sheet and roast in the preheated oven for about 20-25 minutes or until they are tender and slightly caramelized.
c) In a bowl, whisk together eggs, milk, shredded cheddar cheese, salt, and pepper.
d) Heat an oven-safe skillet over medium heat. Pour the egg mixture over the roasted vegetables.
e) Cook on the stove for 2-3 minutes until the edges start to set. Transfer the skillet to the preheated oven and bake for an additional 15-20 minutes or until the frittata is set in the center. Allow the frittata to cool slightly before slicing. Garnish with fresh herbs if desired and serve warm.

NUTRITION PER SERVING: Calories: 280, Protein: 16g, Carbohydrates: 10g, Dietary Fiber: 3g, Fat: 20g, Sodium: 330mg

TIPS: Add sautéed onions or mushrooms for additional flavor.

● Experiment with different cheeses, such as feta or goat cheese.

SMOOTHIES

36. Berry Blast Smoothie

37. Green Goddess Smoothie

38. Tropical Paradise Smoothie

39. Protein Power Smoothie

40. Chocolate Banana Almond Smoothie

41. Orange Creamsicle Smoothie

42. Minty Melon Smoothie

43. Avocado Berry Burst Smoothie

44. Citrus Sunrise Smoothie

45. Blueberry Almond Joy Smoothie

Berry Blast Smoothie

INGREDIENTS:

1 cup mixed berries (strawberries, blueberries, raspberries), 1 banana (peeled and sliced), ½ cup Greek yogurt, ½ cup almond milk (or any preferred milk), 1 tablespoon honey (optional), Ice cubes (optional)

Servings: 2

Preparation Time: 5 minutes

DIRECTIONS:

a) In a blender, combine the mixed berries (sliced) banana, Greek yogurt, almond milk, and honey.
b) If desired, add ice cubes for a colder and thicker consistency.
c) Blend on high speed until smooth and creamy.
d) Taste the smoothie and adjust the sweetness by adding more honey if needed.
e) Pour into glasses and serve immediately.

NUTRITION PER SERVING: Calories: 150, Protein: 6g, Carbohydrates: 30g, Dietary Fiber: 5g, Fat: 2g, Sodium: 50mg

TIPS:

● Add a handful of spinach or kale for a nutrient boost without altering the flavor significantly.
● Include a tablespoon of chia seeds or flaxseeds for added fiber and omega-3 fatty acids.
● Use frozen berries for a colder and thicker smoothie.
● Experiment with different variations of milk, such as coconut milk or soy milk.

Green Goddess Smoothie

INGREDIENTS:

1 cup spinach leaves (washed), ½ cucumber (peeled and sliced), ½ avocado (peeled and pitted), ½ banana (peeled), ½ cup pineapple chunks, 1 cup coconut water (or water), 1 tablespoon chia seeds (optional), Ice cubes (optional)

Servings: 2

Preparation Time: 5 minutes

DIRECTIONS:

a) In a blender, combine the spinach leaves (sliced) cucumber, avocado, banana, pineapple chunks, coconut water, and chia seeds.
b) If desired, add ice cubes for a colder and thicker consistency.
c) Blend on high speed until the smoothie is well combined and has a creamy texture.
d) Taste and adjust the sweetness or thickness by adding more banana or ice if needed.
e) Pour into glasses and serve immediately.

NUTRITION PER SERVING: Calories: 180, Protein: 4g, Carbohydrates: 25g, Dietary Fiber: 8g, Fat: 9g, Sodium: 80mg

TIPS:

- Include a tablespoon of flaxseeds or hemp seeds for added nutritional benefits.
- Squeeze in fresh lemon or lime juice for a citrusy kick.
- Customize the thickness by adjusting the amount of liquid or ice cubes.

Tropical Paradise Smoothie

INGREDIENTS:

1 cup pineapple chunks, ½ cup mango chunks, 1 banana (peeled), ½ cup coconut milk, ½ cup orange juice, 1 tablespoon honey (optional), Ice cubes (optional)

Servings: 2

Preparation Time: 5 minutes

DIRECTIONS:

a) In a blender, combine the pineapple chunks, mango chunks (peeled) banana, coconut milk, orange juice, and honey.
b) If desired, add ice cubes for a colder and thicker consistency.
c) Blend on high speed until the smoothie is well combined and has a creamy texture.
d) Taste and adjust the sweetness by adding more honey if needed.
e) Pour into glasses and serve immediately.

NUTRITION PER SERVING: Calories: 220, Protein: 2g, Carbohydrates: 50g, Dietary Fiber: 5g, Fat: 4g, Sodium: 15mg

TIPS:

● Include a handful of spinach or kale for added nutrients without significantly altering the flavor.
● Add a squeeze of lime juice for a citrusy twist.

Protein Power Smoothie

INGREDIENTS:

1 cup Greek yogurt, ½ cup cottage cheese, 1 scoop protein powder, 1 banana (peeled), 1 tablespoon almond butter, 1 tablespoon chia seeds, 1 cup almond milk (or any preferred milk), Ice cubes (optional)

Servings: 2

Preparation Time: 5optional

DIRECTIONS:

a) In a blender, combine Greek yogurt, cottage cheese, protein powder (peeled) banana, almond butter, chia seeds, and almond milk.
b) If desired, add ice cubes for a colder and thicker consistency.
c) Blend on high speed until the smoothie is well combined and has a creamy texture.
d) Taste and adjust the thickness by adding more milk if needed.
e) Pour into glasses and serve immediately.

NUTRITION PER SERVING: Calories: 400, Protein: 35g, Carbohydrates: 28g, Dietary Fiber: 5g, Fat: 18g, Sodium: 250mg

TIPS:

- Customize the flavor by using different protein powder varieties.
- Include a handful of spinach for added nutrients without altering the taste significantly.
- Add a drizzle of honey or maple syrup if you prefer a sweeter smoothie.
- Use frozen banana slices for a colder and creamier texture.

Chocolate Banana Almond Smoothie

INGREDIENTS:

2 ripe bananas (peeled), 2 tablespoons almond butter, 1 tablespoon cocoa powder, 1 cup almond milk (or any preferred milk), 1 scoop chocolate protein powder (optional), 1 tablespoon honey or maple syrup (optional), Ice cubes (optional)

Servings: 2

Preparation Time: 5 minutes

DIRECTIONS:

a) In a blender, combine ripe bananas, almond butter, cocoa powder, almond milk, chocolate protein powder (if using), and honey or maple syrup (if desired).
b) If desired, add ice cubes for a colder and thicker consistency.
c) Blend on high speed until the smoothie is well combined and has a creamy texture.
d) Taste and adjust the sweetness by adding more honey or maple syrup if needed.
e) Pour into glasses and serve immediately.

NUTRITION PER SERVING: Calories: 300, Protein: 8g, Carbohydrates: 40g, Dietary Fiber: 6g, Fat: 15g, Sodium: 180mg

TIPS:

● Top with a sprinkle of chopped almonds or shaved dark chocolate for added texture.
● Include a handful of spinach for a nutrient boost without significantly affecting the flavor.
● Use frozen banana slices for a thicker and colder smoothie.

Orange Creamsicle Smoothie

INGREDIENTS:

2 large oranges (peeled and segmented), 1 cup Greek yogurt, ½ cup milk (dairy or plant-based), 1 tablespoon honey or maple syrup (optional), 1 teaspoon vanilla extract, Ice cubes (optional)

Servings: 2

Preparation Time: 5 minutes

DIRECTIONS:

a) In a blender, combine the peeled and segmented oranges, Greek yogurt, milk, honey, or maple syrup (if using), and vanilla extract.
b) If desired, add ice cubes for a colder and thicker consistency.
c) Blend on high speed until the smoothie is well combined and has a creamy texture.
d) Taste and adjust the sweetness by adding more honey or maple syrup if needed.
e) Pour into glasses and serve immediately.

NUTRITION PER SERVING: Calories: 200, Protein: 10g, Carbohydrates: 35g, Dietary Fiber: 4g, Fat: 3g, Sodium: 70mg

TIPS:

● Add a scoop of vanilla protein powder for an extra protein boost.
● Garnish with a slice of orange on the rim of the glass for a decorative touch.
● Use frozen orange segments for a colder and creamier smoothie.
● Experiment with different citrus fruits like tangerines or clementines for variety.

Minty Melon Smoothie

INGREDIENTS:

2 cups cubed honeydew melon, 1 cup cubed cantaloupe, ½ cup fresh mint leaves, 1 lime (juiced), 1 tablespoon honey or agave syrup (optional), 1 cup coconut water, Ice cubes (optional)

Servings: 2

Preparation Time: 5 minutes

DIRECTIONS:

a) In a blender, combine the cubed honeydew melon, cubed cantaloupe, fresh mint leaves, lime juice, honey or agave syrup (if using), and coconut water.
b) If desired, add ice cubes for a colder and thicker consistency.
c) Blend on high speed until the smoothie is well combined and has a refreshing texture.
d) Taste and adjust the sweetness by adding more honey or agave syrup if needed.
e) Pour into glasses and serve immediately.

NUTRITION PER SERVING: Calories: 120, Protein: 2g, Carbohydrates: 30g, Dietary Fiber: 3g, Fat: 0g, Sodium: 120mg

TIPS:

● Add a handful of spinach for added nutrients without significantly altering the flavor.
● Garnish with a sprig of fresh mint or a slice of lime for a decorative touch.
● Use frozen melon cubes for a colder and creamier smoothie.
● Experiment with different types of melons, such as watermelon or casaba melon, for variety.

Avocado Berry Burst Smoothie

INGREDIENTS:

½ avocado (peeled and pitted), 1 cup mixed berries (strawberries, blueberries, raspberries), 1 banana (peeled), 1 cup spinach leaves (washed), 1 cup almond milk (or any preferred milk), 1 tablespoon chia seeds, 1 tablespoon honey or maple syrup (optional), Ice cubes (optional)

Servings: 2

Preparation Time: 5 minutes

DIRECTIONS:

a) In a blender, combine the peeled and pitted avocado, mixed berries, banana, spinach leaves, almond milk, chia seeds, and honey or maple syrup (if using).
b) If desired, add ice cubes for a colder and thicker consistency.
c) Blend on high speed until the smoothie is well combined and has a creamy texture.
d) Taste and adjust the sweetness by adding more honey or maple syrup if needed.
e) Pour into glasses and serve immediately.

NUTRITION PER SERVING: Calories: 250, Protein: 5g, Carbohydrates: 40g, Dietary Fiber: 10g, Fat: 10g, Sodium: 120mg

TIPS:

● Add a scoop of vanilla protein powder for an extra protein boost.
● Include a handful of frozen pineapple chunks for a tropical twist.
● Experiment with different greens like kale or arugula for variety.

Citrus Sunrise Smoothie

INGREDIENTS:

1 orange (peeled and segmented), 1 grapefruit (peeled and segmented), 1 cup pineapple chunks, 1 banana (peeled), ½ cup Greek yogurt, 1 tablespoon honey or agave syrup (optional), Ice cubes (optional)

Servings: 2

Preparation Time: 5 minutes

DIRECTIONS:

a) In a blender, combine the orange, grapefruit, pineapple chunks (peeled) banana, Greek yogurt, and honey or agave syrup (if using).
b) If desired, add ice cubes for a colder and thicker consistency.
c) Blend on high speed until the smoothie is well combined and has a refreshing texture.
d) Taste and adjust the sweetness by adding more honey or agave syrup if needed.
e) Pour into glasses and serve immediately.

NUTRITION PER SERVING: Calories: 220, Protein: 5g, Carbohydrates: 50g, Dietary Fiber: 7g, Fat: 1g, Sodium: 20mg

TIPS:

● Include a handful of spinach or kale for added nutrients without significantly altering the flavor.
● Garnish with a slice of orange or grapefruit on the rim of the glass for a decorative touch.
● Use frozen fruit for a colder and creamier smoothie.
● Experiment with different citrus fruits like tangerines or clementines for variety.

Blueberry Almond Joy Smoothie

INGREDIENTS:

1 cup blueberries (fresh or frozen), 1 banana (peeled), 2 tablespoons shredded coconut, 2 tablespoons almond butter, 1 cup almond milk (or any preferred milk), 1 tablespoon cocoa powder, 1 tablespoon honey or maple syrup (optional), Ice cubes (optional)

Servings: 2

Preparation Time: 5 minutes

DIRECTIONS:

a) In a blender, combine the blueberries (peeled) banana, shredded coconut, almond butter, almond milk, cocoa powder, and honey or maple syrup (if using).
b) If desired, add ice cubes for a colder and thicker consistency.
c) Blend on high speed until the smoothie is well combined and has a creamy texture.
d) Taste and adjust the sweetness by adding more honey or maple syrup if needed.
e) Pour into glasses and serve immediately.

NUTRITION PER SERVING: Calories: 300, Protein: 7g, Carbohydrates: 40g, Dietary Fiber: 8g, Fat: 15g, Sodium: 150mg

TIPS:

- Add a handful of spinach for added nutrients without significantly altering the flavor.
- Top with sliced almonds or additional shredded coconut for a crunchy texture.
- Use frozen blueberries for a colder and creamier smoothie.
- Experiment with different nut butter like hazelnut or peanut butter for variety.

SOUPS & STEW

46. Vegetable and Lentil Soup

47. Chicken and Spinach Soup

48. Turmeric Carrot Ginger Soup

49. Quinoa and Vegetable Stew

50. Tomato Basil Soup with Chickpeas

51. Zucchini Noodle Chicken Soup

52. Kale and White Bean Stew

53. Broccoli and Cheddar Soup (using cauliflower for creaminess)

54. Lentil and Mushroom Stew

55. Spinach and Turkey Meatball Soup

56. Butternut Squash and Apple Soup

57. Cauliflower and Leek Soup

58. Split Pea and Ham Soup

Vegetable and Lentil Soup

INGREDIENTS:

1 cup dry lentils (rinsed and drained), 1 onion (chopped), 2 carrots (peeled and diced), 2 celery stalks (diced), 3 cloves garlic (minced), 1 can (14 ounces) diced tomatoes, 6 cups vegetable broth, 2 teaspoons ground cumin, 1 teaspoon ground coriander, 1 teaspoon smoked paprika, Salt and pepper to taste, 2 tablespoons olive oil, Fresh parsley for garnish (optional)

Servings: 6

Cooking Time: 30 minutes

DIRECTIONS:

a) In a large pot, heat olive oil over medium heat. Add chopped onion, carrots, and celery. Sauté until vegetables are softened, about 5 minutes.
b) Add minced garlic and sauté for an additional 1-2 minutes until fragrant.
c) Stir in ground cumin, ground coriander, smoked paprika, salt, and pepper.
d) Add rinsed lentils (diced) tomatoes (with their juices), and vegetable broth to the pot. Bring to a boil.
e) Reduce heat to low, cover the pot, and simmer for 20-25 minutes or until lentils are tender.
f) Adjust seasoning if needed and serve hot.
g) Garnish with fresh parsley if desired.

NUTRITION PER SERVING: Calories: 250, Protein: 14g, Carbohydrates: 40g, Dietary Fiber: 16g, Fat: 4g, Sodium: 800mg

TIPS:

- Add chopped kale or spinach for added greens.
- Include diced potatoes or sweet potatoes for extra heartiness.
- Drizzle with olive oil or top with a dollop of Greek yogurt for richness.

Chicken and Spinach Soup

INGREDIENTS:

1 pound boneless, skinless chicken breasts (diced), 1 onion (finely chopped), 2 carrots (peeled and sliced), 2 celery stalks (diced), 3 cloves garlic (minced), 6 cups chicken broth, 1 can (14 ounces) diced tomatoes, 1 cup small pasta (such as orzo or ditalini), 4 cups fresh spinach leaves (washed), 1 teaspoon dried thyme, 1 teaspoon dried rosemary, Salt and pepper to taste, 2 tablespoons olive oil, Fresh parsley for garnish (optional)

Servings: 6

Cooking Time: 25 minutes

DIRECTIONS:

a) In a large pot, heat olive oil over medium heat. Add chopped onion, carrots, and celery. Sauté until vegetables are softened, about 5 minutes. Add diced chicken to the pot and cook until browned.
b) Stir in minced garlic, dried thyme, dried rosemary, salt, and pepper.
c) Pour in chicken broth (diced) tomatoes (with their juices), and bring to a boil.
d) Add pasta to the pot and simmer for 10-12 minutes or until pasta is cooked.
e) Add fresh spinach leaves to the soup and cook for an additional 2-3 minutes until wilted.
f) Adjust seasoning if needed and serve hot. Garnish with fresh parsley if desired.

NUTRITION PER SERVING: Calories: 300, Protein: 25g, Carbohydrates: 25g, Dietary Fiber: 4g, Fat: 10g, Sodium: 900mg

TIPS: Substitute other pasta shapes like fusilli or farfalle.

*   Include a handful of diced potatoes for extra heartiness.
*   Top with grated Parmesan cheese before serving.

Turmeric Carrot Ginger Soup

INGREDIENTS:

1 pound carrots (peeled and chopped), 1 onion (chopped), 2 inches fresh ginger (peeled and grated), 3 cloves garlic (minced), 1 teaspoon ground turmeric, 6 cups vegetable broth, 1 can (14 ounces) coconut milk, 2 tablespoons olive oil, Salt and pepper to taste, Fresh cilantro for garnish (optional)

Servings: 6

Cooking Time: 25 minutes

DIRECTIONS:

a) In a large pot, heat olive oil over medium heat. Add chopped onion and sauté until translucent.
b) Add grated ginger and minced garlic to the pot. Sauté for an additional 2 minutes until fragrant.
c) Stir in ground turmeric (chopped) carrots, and vegetable broth. Bring to a boil.
d) Reduce heat to low, cover the pot, and simmer for 15-20 minutes or until carrots are tender.
e) Use an immersion blender to puree the soup until smooth. Alternatively, transfer the soup to a blender in batches.
f) Stir in coconut milk and heat through.
g) Season with salt and pepper to taste.
h) Serve hot, garnished with fresh cilantro if desired.

NUTRITION PER SERVING: Calories: 250, Protein: 3g, Carbohydrates: 20g, Dietary Fiber: 5g, Fat: 18g, Sodium: 800mg

TIPS: Top with a dollop of Greek yogurt or coconut cream before serving.

● Garnish with toasted pumpkin seeds or almonds for added crunch.

Quinoa and Vegetable Stew

INGREDIENTS:

1 cup quinoa (rinsed), 1 onion (chopped), 2 carrots (peeled and diced), 2 celery stalks (diced), 1 bell pepper (diced), 3 cloves garlic (minced), 1 zucchini (diced), 1 can (14 ounces) diced tomatoes, 6 cups vegetable broth, 1 teaspoon ground cumin, 1 teaspoon smoked paprika, ½ teaspoon turmeric, Salt and pepper to taste, 2 tablespoons olive oil, Fresh parsley for garnish (optional)

Servings: 6

Cooking Time: 25 minutes

DIRECTIONS:

a) In a large pot, heat olive oil over medium heat. Add chopped onion, carrots, celery, and bell pepper. Sauté until vegetables are softened, about 5 minutes.
b) Add minced garlic, ground cumin, smoked paprika, turmeric, salt, and pepper. Stir well.
c) Add diced zucchini to the pot and continue to sauté for an additional 3-4 minutes.
d) Pour in diced tomatoes (with their juices), vegetable broth, and rinsed quinoa. Bring to a boil.
e) Reduce heat to low, cover the pot, and simmer for 15-20 minutes or until quinoa is cooked and vegetables are tender.
f) Garnish with fresh parsley if desired and serve hot.

NUTRITION PER SERVING: Calories: 300, Protein: 8g, Carbohydrates: 50g, Dietary Fiber: 8g, Fat: 8g, Sodium: 800mg

TIPS: Add a can of chickpeas or black beans for additional protein.

● Top with a dollop of Greek yogurt or a sprinkle of feta cheese.

Tomato Basil Soup with Chickpeas

INGREDIENTS:

1 can (28 ounces) crushed tomatoes, 1 can (15 ounces) chickpeas (drained and rinsed), 1 onion (chopped), 3 cloves garlic (minced), 2 tablespoons tomato paste, 4 cups vegetable broth, 1 cup fresh basil leaves (chopped), 1 teaspoon dried oregano, ½ teaspoon red pepper flakes (optional), Salt and pepper to taste, 2 tablespoons olive oil, Grated Parmesan cheese for garnish (optional)

Servings: 6

Cooking Time: 25 minutes

DIRECTIONS:

a) In a large pot, heat olive oil over medium heat. Add chopped onion and sauté until translucent.
b) Add minced garlic and continue to sauté for an additional 1-2 minutes until fragrant.
c) Stir in tomato paste and cook for 2-3 minutes to enhance the flavor.
d) Add crushed tomatoes, chickpeas, vegetable broth, dried oregano, and red pepper flakes (if using). Bring to a boil. Reduce heat to low, cover the pot, and simmer for 15-20 minutes to allow flavors to meld.
e) Stir in chopped fresh basil and cook for an additional 2-3 minutes.
f) Season with salt and pepper to taste. Serve hot, garnished with grated Parmesan cheese if desired.

NUTRITION PER SERVING: Calories: 220, Protein: 8g, Carbohydrates: 35g, Dietary Fiber: 8g, Fat: 7g, Sodium: 800mg

TIPS: Blend the soup with an immersion blender for a smoother consistency.

- Add a splash of balsamic vinegar for extra depth of flavor.
- Crumble feta cheese or goat cheese on top before serving.

Zucchini Noodle Chicken Soup

INGREDIENTS:

1 pound boneless, skinless chicken breasts (thinly sliced), 2 zucchinis (spiralized into noodles), 1 onion (chopped), 3 carrots (peeled and sliced), 2 celery stalks (diced), 3 cloves garlic (minced), 8 cups chicken broth, 1 teaspoon dried thyme, 1 teaspoon dried rosemary, 1 bay leaf, Salt and pepper to taste, 2 tablespoons olive oil, Fresh parsley for garnish (optional)

Servings: 6

Cooking Time: 25 minutes

DIRECTIONS:

a) In a large pot, heat olive oil over medium heat. Add chopped onion (sliced) carrots, and diced celery. Sauté until vegetables are softened, about 5 minutes.
b) Add thinly sliced chicken to the pot and cook until browned on all sides. Stir in minced garlic, dried thyme, dried rosemary, salt, and pepper. Pour in chicken broth and add the bay leaf. Bring to a boil.
c) Reduce heat to low, cover the pot, and simmer for 15-20 minutes or until chicken is cooked through and vegetables are tender. Add spiralized zucchini noodles to the pot and cook for an additional 3-4 minutes until they are just tender. Adjust seasoning if needed and serve hot. Garnish with fresh parsley if desired.

NUTRITION PER SERVING: Calories: 250, Protein: 25g, Carbohydrates: 10g, Dietary Fiber: 3g, Fat: 12g, Sodium: 900mg

TIPS:

● Substitute other vegetables like spinach or kale for added greens.
● Add a squeeze of fresh lemon juice before serving for a burst of citrus flavor.

Kale and White Bean Stew

INGREDIENTS:

2 cans (15 ounces each) white beans (drained and rinsed), 1 bunch kale (stems removed and leaves chopped), 1 onion (finely chopped), 3 carrots (peeled and diced), 3 celery stalks (diced), 3 cloves garlic (minced), 6 cups vegetable broth, 1 can (14 ounces) diced tomatoes, 2 teaspoons dried thyme, 1 teaspoon dried rosemary, 1 bay leaf, Salt and pepper to taste, 2 tablespoons olive oil, Grated Parmesan cheese for garnish (optional)

Servings: 6

Cooking Time: 25 minutes

DIRECTIONS:

a) Heat olive oil, sauté diced onion, carrots, and celery until softened.
b) Add minced garlic, dried thyme, rosemary, salt, pepper. Pour in vegetable broth, diced tomatoes with juices, and bay leaf. Bring to a boil, then simmer covered for 15-20 minutes.
c) Add chopped kale, simmer for 5-7 minutes until tender.
d) Stir in white beans, heat through.
e) Adjust seasoning, serve hot. Garnish with Parmesan if desired.

NUTRITION PER SERVING: Calories: 300, Protein: 14g, Carbohydrates: 50g, Dietary Fiber: 12g, Fat: 6g, Sodium: 900mg

TIPS: Add a splash of balsamic vinegar for extra depth of flavor.

- Include a pinch of red pepper flakes for a hint of heat.
- Serve over cooked quinoa or brown rice for a heartier meal.
- Drizzle with extra virgin olive oil before serving for richness.

Broccoli and Cheddar Soup with Creamy Cauliflower

INGREDIENTS:

1 pound broccoli (florets separated), 1 cauliflower (chopped) into florets, 1 onion (chopped), 2 carrots (peeled and diced), 3 cloves garlic (minced), 4 cups vegetable broth, 2 cups shredded sharp cheddar cheese, 1 cup milk (dairy or plant-based), 2 tablespoons all-purpose flour, 2 tablespoons butter, Salt and pepper to taste, Olive oil for sautéing, Chopped chives for garnish (optional)

Servings: 6

Cooking Time: 25 minutes

DIRECTIONS:

a) Sauté onions, carrots, and garlic in olive oil until softened (5 min).
b) Add broccoli and cauliflower; sauté for 3-4 more minutes.
c) In a separate saucepan, melt butter, stir in flour, and gradually whisk in vegetable broth to create a smooth mixture.
d) Pour the broth mixture into the pot; simmer for 15-20 minutes until vegetables are tender.
e) Use an immersion blender to puree the soup.
f) Stir in cheddar cheese and milk; cook until melted and heated through.
g) Season with salt and pepper; serve hot, garnished with chopped chives if desired.

NUTRITION PER SERVING: Calories: 300, Protein: 15g, Carbohydrates: 20g, Dietary Fiber: 5g, Fat: 18g, Sodium: 800mg

TIPS: Top with croutons or toasted bread cubes for added crunch.

● Add a pinch of nutmeg for a warm and aromatic flavor.

Lentil and Mushroom Stew

INGREDIENTS:

1 cup dry brown lentils (rinsed), 1 pound mushrooms (sliced), 1 onion (chopped), 3 carrots (peeled and diced), 3 celery stalks (diced), 3 cloves garlic (minced), 6 cups vegetable broth, 1 can (14 ounces) diced tomatoes, 2 teaspoons dried thyme, 1 teaspoon smoked paprika, 1 bay leaf, Salt and pepper to taste, 2 tablespoons olive oil, Fresh parsley for garnish (optional)

Servings: 6

Cooking Time: 30 minutes

DIRECTIONS:

a) In a large pot, heat olive oil over medium heat. Add chopped onion (diced) carrots, and diced celery. Sauté until vegetables are softened, about 5 minutes.
b) Add sliced mushrooms to the pot and cook until they release their moisture and become golden brown.
c) Stir in minced garlic, dried thyme, smoked paprika, salt, and pepper.
d) Add rinsed lentils (diced) tomatoes (with their juices), vegetable broth, and the bay leaf. Bring to a boil.
e) Reduce heat to low, cover the pot, and simmer for 20-25 minutes or until lentils are tender.
f) Adjust seasoning if needed and serve hot.
g) Garnish with fresh parsley if desired.

NUTRITION PER SERVING: Calories: 280, Protein: 15g, Carbohydrates: 40g, Dietary Fiber: 15g, Fat: 6g, Sodium: 800mg

TIPS: Add a splash of balsamic vinegar for extra depth of flavor.

● Top with a dollop of Greek yogurt or a sprinkle of feta cheese.

Spinach and Turkey Meatball Soup

INGREDIENTS:

FOR TURKEY MEATBALLS: 1 pound ground turkey, ½ cup breadcrumbs, ¼ cup grated Parmesan cheese, 1 egg, 2 cloves garlic (minced), 1 teaspoon dried oregano, Salt and pepper to taste

FOR SOUP: 1 onion (chopped), 2 carrots (peeled and sliced), 3 celery stalks (diced), 3 cloves garlic (minced), 6 cups chicken broth, 1 can (14 ounces) diced tomatoes, 4 cups fresh spinach leaves (washed), 1 teaspoon dried thyme, Salt and pepper to taste, Olive oil for sautéing, Fresh parsley for garnish (optional)

Servings: 6

Cooking Time: 25 minutes

DIRECTIONS:

a) Combine ground turkey, breadcrumbs, Parmesan cheese, minced egg, garlic, oregano, salt, and pepper in a large mixing bowl. Shape the mixture into small meatballs and set aside.
b) In a large pot, sauté sliced onion, carrots, and diced celery in olive oil until softened (5 min).
c) Add minced garlic; sauté for an additional 2 minutes. Pour in chicken broth, diced tomatoes with their juices, and dried thyme; bring to a boil. Gently add turkey meatballs; simmer for 15-20 minutes until cooked through. Stir in fresh spinach; cook until wilted. Season with salt and pepper to taste.
d) Serve hot, garnished with fresh parsley if desired.

NUTRITION PER SERVING: Calories: 250, Protein: 20g, Carbohydrates: 15g, Dietary Fiber: 4g, Fat: 12g, Sodium: 900mg

TIPS: Substitute ground chicken or lean beef for the turkey.

● Serve with a slice of crusty bread or a side of rice for a more substantial meal.

Butternut Squash and Apple Soup

INGREDIENTS:

1 butternut squash (peeled, seeded, and diced), 2 apples (peeled, cored, and diced), 1 onion (chopped), 3 cloves garlic (minced), 4 cups vegetable broth, 1 cup apple cider, 1 teaspoon ground cinnamon, ½ teaspoon ground nutmeg, Salt and pepper to taste, 2 tablespoons olive oil, Toasted pumpkin seeds for garnish (optional)

Servings: 6

Cooking Time: 30 minutes

DIRECTIONS:

a) In a large pot, heat olive oil over medium heat. Add chopped onion and sauté until translucent.
b) Add minced garlic and continue to sauté for an additional 2 minutes until fragrant.
c) Add diced butternut squash and apples to the pot. Stir well.
d) Pour in vegetable broth, apple cider, ground cinnamon, ground nutmeg, salt, and pepper. Bring to a boil.
e) Reduce heat to low, cover the pot, and simmer for 20-25 minutes or until butternut squash and apples are tender.
f) Use an immersion blender to puree the soup until smooth. Alternatively, transfer the soup to a blender in batches.
g) Adjust seasoning if needed and serve hot.
h) Garnish with toasted pumpkin seeds if desired.

NUTRITION PER SERVING: Calories: 180, Protein: 2g, Carbohydrates: 40g, Dietary Fiber: 6g, Fat: 3g, Sodium: 600mg

Cauliflower and Leek Soup

INGREDIENTS:

1 head cauliflower (chopped into florets), 2 leeks, white and light green parts (sliced), 1 onion (chopped), 3 cloves garlic (minced), 4 cups vegetable broth, 1 potato (peeled and diced), 2 tablespoons olive oil, 1 teaspoon dried thyme, Salt and pepper to taste, Fresh chives for garnish (optional)

Servings: 6

Cooking Time: 25 minutes

DIRECTIONS:

a) In a large pot, heat olive oil over medium heat. Add chopped onion and leeks. Sauté until softened, about 5 minutes.
b) Add minced garlic and continue to sauté for an additional 2 minutes until fragrant.
c) Add cauliflower florets (diced) potato, dried thyme, salt, and pepper. Stir well.
d) Pour in vegetable broth and bring to a boil. Reduce heat to low, cover the pot, and simmer for 20-25 minutes or until cauliflower and potato are tender.
e) Use an immersion blender to puree the soup until smooth. Alternatively, transfer the soup to a blender in batches. Adjust seasoning if needed and serve hot.
f) Garnish with fresh chives if desired.

NUTRITION PER SERVING: Calories: 120, Protein: 3g, Carbohydrates: 20g, Dietary Fiber: 4g, Fat: 4g, Sodium: 600mg

TIPS: Stir in a splash of milk or cream for added richness.

- Add a pinch of nutmeg for a warm and aromatic flavor.
- Serve with crusty bread or croutons on the side.

Split Pea and Ham Soup

INGREDIENTS:

1 pound dried split peas (rinsed and drained), 1 ham hock or 1 to 1.5 cups diced ham, 1 onion (chopped), 3 carrots (peeled and diced), 3 celery stalks (diced), 3 cloves garlic (minced), 8 cups chicken or ham broth, 1 bay leaf, 1 teaspoon dried thyme, Salt and pepper to taste, 2 tablespoons olive oil, Fresh parsley for garnish (optional)

Servings: 6

Cooking Time: 1.5 to 2 hours

DIRECTIONS:

a) Heat olive oil, sauté diced onion, carrots, and celery until softened (about 5 minutes).
b) Add minced garlic, sauté for an additional 2 minutes until fragrant.
c) Add dried split peas, ham hock (or diced ham), bay leaf, dried thyme, salt, and pepper. Stir well.
d) Pour in chicken or ham broth, bring to a boil. Reduce heat, cover, and simmer for 1.5 to 2 hours until split peas are tender. If using ham hock, remove, shred meat, and return to soup. Discard ham hock bone.
e) Adjust seasoning, serve hot. Garnish with fresh parsley if desired.

NUTRITION PER SERVING: Calories: 300, Protein: 20g, Carbohydrates: 50g, Dietary Fiber: 16g, Fat: 5g, Sodium: 900mg

TIPS: For a smoother consistency, use an immersion blender to partially blend the soup.

- Add a splash of apple cider vinegar for a tangy kick.
- Enjoy with a slice of crusty bread or cornbread on the side.

MEAT & POULTRY

59. Baked Garlic Parmesan Turkey Meatballs

60. Lemon Dill Roasted Chicken Drumsticks

61. Pesto Grilled Chicken Skewers

62. Mediterranean Turkey Burgers

63. Almond-Crusted Chicken Tenders

64. Baked Salmon with Dill and Lemon

65. Garlic Herb Grilled Lamb Chops

66. Teriyaki Turkey Stir-Fry

67. Lemon Pepper Baked Cod

68. Spiced Chicken Kabobs

69. Balsamic Glazed Pork Tenderloin

70. Rosemary Garlic Roast Beef

71. Garlic Rosemary Pork Chops

Baked Garlic Parmesan Turkey Meatballs

INGREDIENTS:

1 pound ground turkey, ½ cup breadcrumbs, ⅓ cup grated Parmesan cheese, 2 cloves garlic (minced), ¼ cup fresh parsley (chopped), 1 egg, 1 teaspoon dried oregano, ½ teaspoon dried basil, Salt and pepper to taste, Olive oil for greasing, Marinara sauce for serving (optional)

Servings: Approximately 4 servings (4-5 meatballs per serving)

Baking Time: 20-25optional

DIRECTIONS:

a) Preheat the oven to 400°F (200°C). Grease a baking sheet with olive oil.
b) In a large mixing bowl, combine ground turkey, breadcrumbs (grated) Parmesan cheese (minced) garlic (chopped) fresh parsley, egg, dried oregano, dried basil, salt, and pepper. Mix until well combined.
c) Shape the mixture into meatballs, about 1 to 1.5 inches in diameter, and place them on the prepared baking sheet. Bake in the preheated oven for 20-25 minutes or until the meatballs are cooked through and golden brown on the outside. Optionally, serve the meatballs with marinara sauce for dipping or as a topping. Garnish with additional Parmesan cheese and fresh parsley if desired.

NUTRITION PER SERVING: Calories: 250, Protein: 30g, Carbohydrates: 10g, Dietary Fiber: 1g, Fat: 11g, Sodium: 400mg

TIPS:

- Serve the meatballs over spaghetti or your favorite pasta.
- Make a double batch and freeze extra meatballs for a quick and convenient meal.
- Use a combination of ground turkey and ground chicken for a different flavor profile.

Lemon Dill Roasted Chicken Drumsticks

INGREDIENTS:

8 chicken drumsticks, 2 lemons (juiced and zested), 3 tablespoons olive oil, 2 tablespoons fresh dill (chopped), 3 cloves garlic (minced), 1 teaspoon Dijon mustard, Salt and pepper to taste, Lemon slices for garnish (optional), Fresh dill for garnish (optional)

Servings: 4

Marinating Time: 30 minutes to 4 hours

Roasting Time: 40-45 minutes

DIRECTIONS:

a) Whisk lemon juice, zest, olive oil, fresh dill, minced garlic, Dijon mustard, salt, and pepper for marinade.
b) Place chicken drumsticks in a dish or bag, pour marinade over, and refrigerate for 30 mins to 4 hours.
c) Preheat oven to 400°F (200°C). Line baking sheet with parchment paper.
d) Arrange marinated drumsticks on prepared baking sheet.
e) Roast for 40-45 minutes until internal temperature is 165°F (74°C) and skin is crispy.
f) Remove from oven, let chicken rest briefly.
g) Garnish with lemon slices and fresh dill if desired.

NUTRITION PER SERVING: Calories: 350, Protein: 28g, Carbohydrates: 4g, Dietary Fiber: 1g, Fat: 25g, Sodium: 300mg

TIPS: Add a pinch of red pepper flakes for a touch of heat.

● Grill the marinated drumsticks for a different flavor profile.
● Double the marinade and reserve some for basting during the roasting process.

Pesto Grilled Chicken Skewers

INGREDIENTS:

1.5 pounds boneless, skinless chicken breasts (cubed), ½ cup pesto sauce, 2 tablespoons olive oil, 1 tablespoon lemon juice, 2 cloves garlic (minced), Salt and pepper to taste, Wooden or metal skewers

Servings: 4

Marinating Time: 30 minutes to 4 hours

Grilling Time: 10-12 minutes

DIRECTIONS:

a) If using wooden skewers, soak them in water for at least 30 minutes to prevent burning.
b) In a bowl, mix together pesto sauce, olive oil, lemon juice (minced) garlic, salt, and pepper to create the marinade.
c) Thread chicken cubes onto the skewers, leaving a small space between each piece.
d) Place the skewers in a shallow dish and brush them with the pesto marinade. Allow them to marinate in the refrigerator for 30 minutes to 4 hours. Preheat the grill to medium-high heat.
e) Grill the skewers for 10-12 minutes, turning occasionally, until the chicken is cooked through and has a nice char. Remove from the grill and let them rest for a few minutes before serving.

NUTRITION PER SERVING: Calories: 300, Protein: 30g, Carbohydrates: 3g, Dietary Fiber: 1g, Fat: 18g, Sodium: 400mg

TIPS: Serve the skewers with a side of rice, quinoa, or a fresh salad.

- Add cherry tomatoes, bell peppers, or red onion chunks between the chicken cubes on the skewers.
- Drizzle extra pesto over the skewers before serving for added flavor.

Mediterranean Turkey Burgers

INGREDIENTS:

1.5 pounds ground turkey, ½ cup feta cheese (crumbled), ⅓ cup Kalamata olives (chopped), ¼ cup sun-dried tomatoes (chopped), 2 cloves garlic (minced), 1 teaspoon dried oregano, 1 teaspoon dried basil, Salt and pepper to taste, 4 whole grain burger buns, Tzatziki sauce for serving, Lettuce, tomato, and red onion for garnish

Servings: 4

Cooking Time: 10-12 minutes

DIRECTIONS:

a) Preheat the grill or stovetop grill pan to medium-high heat.
b) In a large mixing bowl, combine ground turkey (crumbled) feta cheese (chopped) Kalamata olives (chopped) sun-dried tomatoes (minced) garlic, dried oregano, dried basil, salt, and pepper. Mix until well combined. Divide the mixture into 4 portions and shape them into burger patties.
c) Grill the turkey burgers for 5-6 minutes per side, or until they reach an internal temperature of 165°F (74°C) and are no longer pink in the center.
d) Toast the whole grain burger buns on the grill for 1-2 minutes.
e) Assemble the burgers by placing each turkey patty on a bun. Top with lettuce, tomato, red onion, and a dollop of tzatziki sauce. Serve hot and enjoy!

NUTRITION PER SERVING: Calories: 350, Protein: 30g, Carbohydrates: 25g, Dietary Fiber: 4g, Fat: 15g, Sodium: 600mg

TIPS:

● Use whole grain or lettuce wraps instead of traditional burger buns for a lighter option.
● Customize with your favorite Mediterranean-inspired toppings such as cucumber, feta, or hummus.

Almond-Crusted Chicken Tenders

INGREDIENTS:

1.5 pounds chicken tenders, 1 cup almonds (finely ground), ½ cup whole wheat flour, 2 teaspoons smoked paprika, 1 teaspoon garlic powder, ½ teaspoon salt, ¼ teaspoon black pepper, 2 eggs, Cooking spray or olive oil for baking

Servings: 4

Baking Time: 15-20 minutes

DIRECTIONS:

a) Preheat oven to 425°F (220°C). Line and lightly grease a baking sheet with parchment paper.
b) In a shallow dish, combine finely ground almonds, whole wheat flour, smoked paprika, garlic powder, salt, and black pepper. Mix well. In another shallow dish, whisk eggs.
c) Dip each chicken tender in whisked eggs, coat in almond mixture, pressing the coating onto the chicken.
d) Place coated chicken tenders on the prepared baking sheet.
e) Lightly spray tenders with cooking spray or drizzle with olive oil.
f) Bake in the preheated oven for 15-20 minutes until chicken is cooked and coating is golden brown and crispy. Serve hot with your favorite dipping sauce.

NUTRITION PER SERVING: Calories: 300, Protein: 30g, Carbohydrates: 12g, Dietary Fiber: 4g, Fat: 15g, Sodium: 400mg

TIPS: Use almond meal or almond flour if you prefer a finer texture for the coating.

- Serve with a side of roasted vegetables or a fresh green salad.
- Pair with a dipping sauce like honey mustard, Greek yogurt ranch, or tzatziki.

Baked Salmon with Dill and Lemon

INGREDIENTS:

4 salmon fillets, 2 tablespoons olive oil, 2 tablespoons fresh dill (chopped), Zest of 1 lemon, Juice of 1 lemon, 2 cloves garlic (minced), Salt and pepper to taste, Lemon slices for garnish (optional)

Servings: 4

Baking Time: 12-15 minutes

DIRECTIONS:

a) Preheat the oven to 400°F (200°C). Line a baking sheet with parchment paper.
b) Place the salmon fillets on the prepared baking sheet.
c) In a small bowl, whisk together olive oil (chopped) fresh dill, lemon zest, lemon juice (minced) garlic, salt, and pepper.
d) Brush the salmon fillets with the dill and lemon mixture, ensuring they are well-coated.
e) Bake in the preheated oven for 12-15 minutes, or until the salmon is cooked through and flakes easily with a fork.
f) If desired, garnish with lemon slices before serving.

NUTRITION PER SERVING: Calories: 300, Protein: 25g, Carbohydrates: 2g, Dietary Fiber: 0g, Fat: 20g, Sodium: 300mg

TIPS: Serve the baked salmon with a side of roasted vegetables or steamed asparagus.

● Drizzle a bit of extra olive oil over the salmon before baking for added richness.
● Sprinkle with a pinch of smoked paprika for a smoky flavor.
● Finish with a squeeze of fresh lemon juice before serving for extra brightness.

Garlic Herb Grilled Lamb Chops

INGREDIENTS:

8 lamb chops (about 2 pounds), 3 tablespoons olive oil, 4 cloves garlic (minced), 1 tablespoon fresh rosemary (chopped), 1 tablespoon fresh thyme leaves, Zest of 1 lemon, Juice of 1 lemon, Salt and black pepper to taste

Servings: 4

Marinating Time: 30 minutes to 2 hours

Grilling Time: 8-10 minutes

DIRECTIONS:

a) Combine minced garlic, chopped rosemary, thyme, lemon zest, lemon juice, salt, and black pepper in a bowl for the marinade. Pat lamb chops dry, place in a shallow dish, and brush both sides with the marinade. Cover and refrigerate for 30 minutes to 2 hours.
b) Preheat the grill to medium-high heat. Bring lamb chops to room temperature for 15 minutes.
c) Grill for 4-5 minutes per side for medium-rare or adjust for desired doneness. Remove from the grill and let lamb chops rest before serving.

NUTRITION PER SERVING: Calories: 400, Protein: 35g, Carbohydrates: 2g, Dietary Fiber: 0g, Fat: 28g, Sodium: 150mg

TIPS:

● Serve the grilled lamb chops with a side of mint sauce or a balsamic reduction.
● Include additional herbs like mint or parsley in the marinade for extra freshness.
● Pair with roasted potatoes or a Mediterranean couscous salad.

Teriyaki Turkey Stir-Fry

INGREDIENTS:

1 pound turkey breast (thinly sliced), 2 cups broccoli florets, 1 bell pepper (thinly sliced), 1 carrot (julienned), 1 cup snap peas (trimmed), 3 tablespoons soy sauce, 2 tablespoons teriyaki sauce, 1 tablespoon hoisin sauce, 1 tablespoon sesame oil, 2 tablespoons vegetable oil, 2 cloves garlic (minced), 1 tablespoon ginger (grated), Cooked white or brown rice for serving, Sesame seeds and green onions for garnish (optional)

Servings: 4

Cooking Time: 15 minutes

DIRECTIONS:

a) In a bowl, mix soy sauce, teriyaki sauce, hoisin sauce, and sesame oil to create the sauce. Set aside.
b) Heat vegetable oil in a wok or large skillet over medium-high heat.
c) Add minced garlic and grated ginger to the hot oil, and stir for about 30 seconds until fragrant.
d) Add sliced turkey to the wok and stir-fry until browned and cooked through.
e) Add broccoli, bell pepper, carrot, and snap peas to the wok. Continue to stir-fry for an additional 3-4 minutes until vegetables are tender-crisp. Pour the prepared sauce over the turkey and vegetables, stirring to coat evenly. Cook for an additional 1-2 minutes.
f) Serve the teriyaki turkey stir-fry over cooked rice. Garnish with sesame seeds and chopped green onions.

NUTRITION PER SERVING: Calories: 350, Protein: 30g, Carbohydrates: 25g, Dietary Fiber: 4g, Fat: 15g, Sodium: 900mg

TIPS: Add sliced mushrooms, water chestnuts, or baby corn for extra texture and flavor.

- Substitute turkey with chicken or tofu for a different protein option.
- Use a mix of colorful bell peppers for a visually appealing stir-fry.

Lemon Pepper Baked Cod

INGREDIENTS:

4 cod fillets (about 6
ounces each), 2 tablespoons olive oil, 2 tablespoons lemon juice, 1 teaspoon lemon zest, 1 teaspoon
black pepper, 1 teaspoon dried thyme, 1 teaspoon garlic powder, ½ teaspoon salt, Lemon slices for
garnish (optional), Fresh parsley for garnish (optional)

Servings: 4

Baking Time: 15-20 minutes

DIRECTIONS:

a) Preheat the oven to 400°F (200°C). Line a baking sheet with parchment paper.
b) Place the cod fillets on the prepared baking sheet.
c) In a small bowl, whisk together olive oil, lemon juice, lemon zest, black pepper, dried thyme, garlic powder, and salt.
d) Brush the cod fillets with the lemon pepper mixture, ensuring they are well-coated.
e) Bake in the preheated oven for 15-20 minutes, or until the cod is opaque and flakes easily with a fork.
f) Optional: Garnish with lemon slices and fresh parsley before serving.

NUTRITION PER SERVING: Calories: 200, Protein: 25g, Carbohydrates: 1g, Dietary Fiber: 0g, Fat: 10g, Sodium: 400mg

TIPS: Serve the lemon pepper baked cod with a side of roasted vegetables or steamed asparagus.

- Sprinkle with a pinch of smoked paprika for additional flavor.
- Pair with a light salad or couscous for a complete meal.

Spiced Chicken Kabobs

INGREDIENTS:

1.5 pounds boneless skinless chicken breasts (cubed), 1 red bell pepper (cut into chunks), 1 yellow bell pepper (cut into chunks), 1 red onion, cut into wedges, 1 zucchini (sliced), 3 tablespoons olive oil, 2 teaspoons ground cumin, 2 teaspoons ground coriander, 1 teaspoon smoked paprika, 1 teaspoon garlic powder, 1 teaspoon onion powder, Salt and black pepper to taste

Servings: 4

Marinating Time: 30 minutes to 4 hours

Grilling Time: 10-12 minutes

DIRECTIONS:

a) If using wooden skewers, soak them in water for at least 30 minutes to prevent burning.
b) In a bowl, mix together olive oil, ground cumin, ground coriander, smoked paprika, garlic powder, onion powder, salt, and black pepper to create the spice marinade. Thread the chicken cubes and assorted vegetables onto the skewers, alternating as desired. Place the skewers in a shallow dish and brush them with the spice marinade. Allow them to marinate in the refrigerator for 30 minutes to 4 hours.
c) Preheat the grill to medium-high heat.
d) Grill the chicken kabobs for 5-6 minutes per side, or until the chicken is cooked through and has a nice char. Remove from the grill and let them rest for a few minutes before serving.

NUTRITION PER SERVING: Calories: 300, Protein: 30g, Carbohydrates: 10g, Dietary Fiber: 3g, Fat: 15g, Sodium: 400mg
TIPS: Serve the spiced chicken kabobs with a side of couscous or quinoa.

● Make a yogurt-based dipping sauce with a dash of lemon juice and fresh herbs.

Balsamic Glazed Pork Tenderloin

INGREDIENTS:

2 pork tenderloins (about 1.5 pounds each), ½ cup balsamic vinegar, ¼ cup honey, 2 tablespoons soy sauce, 2 cloves garlic (minced), 1 teaspoon Dijon mustard, 1 teaspoon dried rosemary, Salt and black pepper to taste, 1 tablespoon olive oil

Servings: 6

Marinating Time: 30 minutes to 4 hours

Cooking Time: 20-25 minutes

DIRECTIONS:

a) Whisk balsamic vinegar, honey, soy sauce, minced garlic, Dijon mustard, dried rosemary, salt, and black pepper for the marinade. Place pork tenderloins in a dish or bag, pour half of the marinade over, reserve the other half. Marinate for 30 mins to 4 hours in the refrigerator.
b) Preheat oven to 400°F (200°C). Let pork come to room temperature for 15 minutes.
c) Heat olive oil in an oven-safe skillet over medium-high heat.
d) Sear pork tenderloins on all sides until browned. Brush reserved marinade over the pork.
e) Transfer skillet to the preheated oven, roast for 20-25 minutes or until internal temperature reaches 145°F (63°C), basting occasionally.
f) Remove from the oven, let pork rest for 5 minutes before slicing.

NUTRITION PER SERVING: Calories: 300, Protein: 30g, Carbohydrates: 15g, Dietary Fiber: 0.5g, Fat: 12g, Sodium: 500mg

TIPS: Drizzle extra balsamic glaze over the sliced pork before serving.

● Add a pinch of red pepper flakes to the marinade for a hint of heat.

Rosemary Garlic Roast Beef

INGREDIENTS:

3-4 pounds beef roast (such as sirloin or ribeye), 4 cloves garlic (minced), 2 tablespoons fresh rosemary (chopped), 2 tablespoons olive oil, 1 tablespoon Dijon mustard, 1 teaspoon dried thyme, Salt and black pepper to taste

Servings: 6-8

Marinating Time: 1-2 hours

Roasting Time: 1.5 to 2 hours

DIRECTIONS:

a) Preheat the oven to 325°F (163°C).
b) In a bowl, mix together minced garlic (chopped) fresh rosemary, olive oil, Dijon mustard, dried thyme, salt, and black pepper to create the marinade.
c) Rub the beef roast with the marinade, ensuring it is well-coated. Let it marinate in the refrigerator for 1-2 hours. Place the marinated roast on a rack in a roasting pan.
d) Roast in the preheated oven for 1.5 to 2 hours, or until the internal temperature reaches your desired level of doneness (145°F/63°C for medium-rare, 160°F/71°C for medium).
e) Let the roast beef rest for at least 15 minutes before slicing.

NUTRITION PER SERVING: Calories: 400, Protein: 40g, Carbohydrates: 1g, Dietary Fiber: 0g, Fat: 26g, Sodium: 600mg

TIPS: Baste the roast with its juices during the roasting process for added flavor.

● Add red wine or beef broth to the roasting pan for a flavorful jus.
● Serve with roasted vegetables, mashed potatoes, or a green salad.

Garlic Rosemary Pork Chops

INGREDIENTS:

4 bone-in pork chops (about 1 inch thick), 4 cloves garlic (minced), 2 tablespoons fresh rosemary (chopped), 2 tablespoons olive oil, 1 tablespoon Dijon mustard, 1 tablespoon balsamic vinegar, Salt and black pepper to taste

Servings: 4

Marinating Time: 30 minutes to 2 hours

Cooking Time: 15-20 minutes

DIRECTIONS:

a) In a bowl, mix together minced garlic (chopped) fresh rosemary, olive oil, Dijon mustard, balsamic vinegar, salt, and black pepper to create the marinade.
b) Pat the pork chops dry with paper towels and place them in a shallow dish. Brush both sides of the chops with the marinade. Cover and let the pork chops marinate in the refrigerator for at least 30 minutes, or up to 2 hours for more flavor.
c) Preheat the grill or a stovetop grill pan to medium-high heat. Grill the pork chops for 7-10 minutes per side, or until the internal temperature reaches 145°F (63°C) for medium-rare, or 160°F (71°C) for medium.
d) Remove from the grill and let the pork chops rest for a few minutes before serving.

NUTRITION PER SERVING: Calories: 350, Protein: 30g, Carbohydrates: 2g, Dietary Fiber: 0g, Fat: 25g, Sodium: 300mg

TIPS: Use boneless pork chops if preferred, adjusting the cooking time accordingly.

● Grill some lemon slices alongside the pork chops and squeeze fresh lemon juice over them before serving.

FISH & SEAFOOD

72. Pan-Seared Halibut with Tomato Basil Relish

73. Grilled Lemon Garlic Shrimp Skewers

74. Cilantro Lime Grilled Halibut

75. Garlic Parmesan Baked Shrimp

76. Sesame Ginger Glazed Salmon

77. Lemon Dill Baked Snapper

80. Cajun Blackened Catfish

81. Grilled Swordfish with Tomato Salsa

82. Baked Lemon Herb Scallops

83. Coconut Curry Shrimp

84. Lime Cilantro Grilled Mahi-Mahi

85. Lemon Garlic Baked Salmon

Pan-Seared Halibut with Tomato Basil Relish

INGREDIENTS:

FOR HALIBUT: 4 halibut fillets (6 ounces each), 2 tablespoons olive oil, Salt and black pepper to taste, 1 teaspoon garlic powder, 1 teaspoon lemon zest, 2 tablespoons lemon juice,

FOR TOMATO BASIL RELISH: 1 cup cherry tomatoes (halved), ¼ cup fresh basil (chopped), 2 tablespoons red onion (finely chopped), 2 tablespoons balsamic vinegar, 2 tablespoons extra-virgin olive oil, Salt and black pepper to taste

Servings: 4

Cooking Time: 10 minutes

DIRECTIONS:

FOR HALIBUT:

a) Pat dry halibut fillets. Mix olive oil, salt, pepper, garlic powder, lemon zest, and juice.
b) Brush fillets with the mixture. Cook in a heated non-stick skillet for 3-4 mins per side.

FOR TOMATO BASIL RELISH:

c) Combine chopped cherry tomatoes, basil, red onion, balsamic vinegar, olive oil, salt, and pepper.
d) Spoon over pan-seared halibut fillets.

NUTRITION PER SERVING: Calories: 300, Protein: 30g, Carbohydrates: 6g, Dietary Fiber: 1g, Fat: 18g, Sodium: 300mg

TIPS: Serve the halibut over a bed of quinoa, rice, or couscous.

● Customize the tomato basil relish with additional herbs like parsley or mint.
● Garnish with pine nuts or chopped almonds for added crunch.

Cilantro Lime Grilled Halibut

INGREDIENTS:

4 halibut fillets (6 ounces each), ¼ cup fresh cilantro (chopped), 3 tablespoons olive oil, 3 tablespoons lime juice, 2 cloves garlic (minced), 1 teaspoon ground cumin, Salt and black pepper to taste, Lime wedges for serving

Servings: 4

Grilling Time: 8-10 minutes

DIRECTIONS:

a) In a bowl, combine chopped cilantro, olive oil, lime juice (minced) garlic, ground cumin, salt, and black pepper to create the marinade.
b) Pat the halibut fillets dry with paper towels and place them in a shallow dish. Pour the cilantro lime marinade over the fillets, ensuring they are well-coated. Marinate in the refrigerator for 30 minutes.
c) Preheat the grill to medium-high heat.
d) Remove the halibut from the refrigerator and let it come to room temperature for about 15 minutes.
e) Grill the halibut fillets for 4-5 minutes per side, or until the fish is opaque and easily flakes with a fork.
f) Serve the grilled halibut with lime wedges for an extra burst of citrus flavor.

NUTRITION PER SERVING: Calories: 250, Protein: 30g, Carbohydrates: 2g, Dietary Fiber: 0.5g, Fat: 14g, Sodium: 300mg

TIPS: Garnish with additional fresh cilantro before serving for a vibrant touch.

● Serve the grilled halibut over a bed of rice or alongside quinoa.

Garlic Parmesan Baked Shrimp

INGREDIENTS:

1 pound large shrimp (peeled and deveined), 3 tablespoons unsalted butter (melted), 3 tablespoons olive oil, 4 cloves garlic (minced), ½ cup grated Parmesan cheese, ¼ cup fresh parsley (chopped), 1 teaspoon lemon zest, Salt and black pepper to taste, Lemon wedges for serving

Servings: 4

Baking Time: 12-15 minutes

DIRECTIONS:

a) Preheat the oven to 425°F (220°C).
b) In a bowl, combine melted butter, olive oil (minced) garlic (grated) Parmesan cheese (chopped) fresh parsley, lemon zest, salt, and black pepper.
c) Place the peeled and deveined shrimp in a baking dish in a single layer.
d) Pour the garlic Parmesan mixture over the shrimp, ensuring they are well-coated.
e) Bake in the preheated oven for 12-15 minutes, or until the shrimp are opaque and cooked through.
f) Optional: Broil for an additional 1-2 minutes for a golden brown top.
g) Serve the garlic Parmesan baked shrimp with lemon wedges.

NUTRITION PER SERVING: Calories: 250, Protein: 25g, Carbohydrates: 2g, Dietary Fiber: 0g, Fat: 16g, Sodium: 400mg

TIPS:

● Serve the baked shrimp over pasta or with crusty bread for a complete meal.
● Experiment with different cheese varieties like Pecorino or Asiago for a unique flavor.

Sesame Ginger Glazed Salmon

INGREDIENTS:

4 salmon fillets, 3 tablespoons soy sauce, 2 tablespoons honey, 1 tablespoon sesame oil, 1 tablespoon rice vinegar, 1 tablespoon fresh ginger (grated), 2 cloves garlic (minced), 1 tablespoon sesame seeds (for garnish), Sliced green onions (for garnish), Cooked white or brown rice (optional, for serving)

Servings: 4

Marinating Time: 30 minutes

Cooking Time: 10-12 minutes

DIRECTIONS:

a) In a bowl, whisk together soy sauce, honey, sesame oil, rice vinegar (grated) ginger, and minced garlic to create the marinade. Place the salmon fillets in a shallow dish and pour half of the marinade over them, reserving the other half for later. Let the salmon marinate in the refrigerator for 30 minutes.
b) Preheat the oven to 400°F (200°C).
c) Heat a non-stick skillet over medium-high heat. Sear the salmon fillets for 2-3 minutes per side, or until golden brown. Transfer the seared salmon to a baking sheet and brush with the reserved marinade.
d) Bake in the preheated oven for 8-10 minutes, or until the salmon is cooked through and flakes easily.
e) Garnish with sesame seeds and sliced green onions.
f) Serve the sesame ginger glazed salmon over cooked rice if desired.

NUTRITION PER SERVING: Calories: 350, Protein: 30g, Carbohydrates: 15g, Dietary Fiber: 0.5g, Fat: 18g, Sodium: 600mg

TIPS: Sprinkle with chopped cilantro or parsley for a burst of freshness.

- Serve with steamed broccoli or stir-fried vegetables on the side.
- Substitute brown sugar for honey if preferred.

Lemon Dill Baked Snapper

INGREDIENTS:

4 snapper fillets, 2 tablespoons olive oil, 3 tablespoons fresh lemon juice, 1 tablespoon fresh dill (chopped), 2 cloves garlic (minced), 1 teaspoon lemon zest, Salt and black pepper to taste, Lemon slices for garnish, Fresh dill for garnish

Servings: 4

Baking Time: 15-20 minutes

DIRECTIONS:

a) Preheat the oven to 375°F (190°C).
b) Place the snapper fillets in a baking dish.
c) In a bowl, whisk together olive oil, fresh lemon juice (chopped) fresh dill (minced) garlic, lemon zest, salt, and black pepper.
d) Pour the lemon dill mixture over the snapper fillets, ensuring they are well-coated.
e) Bake in the preheated oven for 15-20 minutes, or until the snapper is cooked through and flakes easily with a fork. Optional: Broil for an additional 1-2 minutes for a golden brown top.
f) Garnish with lemon slices and fresh dill before serving.

NUTRITION PER SERVING: Calories: 200, Protein: 30g, Carbohydrates: 2g, Dietary Fiber: 0.5g, Fat: 8g, Sodium: 300mg

TIPS: Serve the lemon dill baked snapper over a bed of quinoa or rice.

- Include capers or chopped Kalamata olives for added flavor.
- Pair with a side of roasted vegetables or a green salad.

Grilled Lemon Garlic Shrimp Skewers

INGREDIENTS:

1.5 pounds large shrimp (peeled and deveined), 3 tablespoons olive oil, 3 cloves garlic (minced), Zest of 1 lemon, Juice of 1 lemon, 1 teaspoon dried oregano, 1 teaspoon smoked paprika, Salt and pepper to taste, Wooden or metal skewers

Servings: 4

Marinating Time: 15-30 minutes

Grilling Time: 5-7 minutes

DIRECTIONS:

a) If using wooden skewers, soak them in water for at least 15 minutes to prevent burning.
b) In a bowl, whisk together olive oil (minced) garlic, lemon zest, lemon juice, dried oregano, smoked paprika, salt, and pepper to create the marinade.
c) Thread the shrimp onto the skewers, leaving a small space between each shrimp.
d) Place the skewers in a shallow dish and brush them with the marinade. Marinate them for 15-30 minutes.
e) Preheat the grill to medium-high heat.
f) Grill the shrimp skewers for 2-3 minutes per side, or until the shrimp are opaque and lightly charred.
g) Remove from the grill and serve immediately.

NUTRITION PER SERVING: Calories: 200, Protein: 25g, Carbohydrates: 2g, Dietary Fiber: 0g, Fat: 10g, Sodium: 300mg

TIPS: Serve the grilled shrimp skewers over a bed of quinoa, rice, or a fresh salad.

● Garnish with chopped fresh parsley or cilantro for added freshness.

Cajun Blackened Catfish

INGREDIENTS:

4 catfish fillets, 2 tablespoons olive oil, 1 tablespoon paprika, 1 teaspoon dried thyme, 1 teaspoon dried oregano, 1 teaspoon onion powder, 1 teaspoon garlic powder, 1 teaspoon cayenne pepper, 1 teaspoon black pepper, 1 teaspoon white pepper, 1 teaspoon salt, Lemon wedges for serving

Servings: 4

Cooking Time: 8-10 minutes

DIRECTIONS:

a) Preheat a cast-iron skillet over high heat until smoking hot.
b) In a bowl, mix paprika, dried thyme, dried oregano, onion powder, garlic powder, cayenne pepper, black pepper, white pepper, and salt to create the blackening seasoning.
c) Brush each catfish fillet with olive oil on both sides.
d) Coat each fillet generously with the blackening seasoning, pressing the seasoning onto the fish.
e) Place the catfish fillets in the hot skillet and cook for 4-5 minutes on each side, or until the fish is blackened and cooked through.
f) Optional: Finish cooking in a preheated oven at 375°F (190°C) for an additional 3-5 minutes.
g) Serve the Cajun blackened catfish with lemon wedges.

NUTRITION PER SERVING: Calories: 250, Protein: 30g, Carbohydrates: 2g, Dietary Fiber: 1g, Fat: 12g, Sodium: 800mg

TIPS: Adjust the amount of cayenne pepper according to your spice preference.

● Serve with a side of coleslaw, hushpuppies, or cornbread.

Grilled Swordfish with Tomato Salsa

INGREDIENTS:

FOR SWORDFISH: 4 swordfish steaks, 2 tablespoons olive oil, 1 tablespoon lemon juice, 1 teaspoon dried oregano, 1 teaspoon garlic powder, Salt and black pepper to taste

FOR TOMATO SALSA: 1 cup cherry tomatoes (diced), ¼ cup red onion (finely chopped), ¼ cup fresh cilantro (chopped), 1 tablespoon lime juice, 1 tablespoon olive oil, Salt and black pepper to taste

Servings: 4

Marinating Time: 30 minutes

Grilling Time: 8-10 minutes

DIRECTIONS:

a) Mix olive oil, lemon juice, dried oregano, garlic powder, salt, and black pepper in a bowl.
b) Brush swordfish steaks with the marinade and marinate in the refrigerator for 30 minutes.
c) Preheat the grill to medium-high heat.
d) Grill swordfish for 4-5 minutes per side until cooked through with grill marks.
e) In another bowl, combine diced cherry tomatoes, red onion, fresh cilantro, lime juice, olive oil, salt, and black pepper. Add jalapeño if desired. Mix well.
f) Place grilled swordfish steaks on serving plates.
g) Spoon tomato salsa over each swordfish steak.
h) Optional: Garnish with cilantro and serve with lime wedges.

NUTRITION PER SERVING: Calories: 300, Protein: 30g, Carbohydrates: 5g, Dietary Fiber: 1.5g, Fat: 18g, Sodium: 500mg

TIPS: Experiment with different herbs in the marinade, such as thyme or rosemary.

Baked Lemon Herb Scallops

INGREDIENTS:

1 pound fresh scallops, 2 tablespoons olive oil, 2 tablespoons fresh lemon juice, 1 teaspoon lemon zest, 2 cloves garlic (minced), 1 tablespoon fresh parsley (chopped), 1 teaspoon dried thyme, Salt and black pepper to taste, ¼ cup breadcrumbs (optional, for topping)

Servings: 4

Baking Time: 12-15 minutes

DIRECTIONS:

a) Preheat the oven to 375°F (190°C).
b) If the scallops are large, you can cut them into smaller pieces for even cooking.
c) In a bowl, mix together olive oil, fresh lemon juice, lemon zest (minced) garlic (chopped) fresh parsley, dried thyme, salt, and black pepper.
d) Add the scallops to the bowl and toss them in the lemon herb mixture until well-coated.
e) Place the scallops in a baking dish in a single layer. Optional: Sprinkle breadcrumbs over the top for added texture. Bake in the preheated oven for 12-15 minutes, or until the scallops are opaque and lightly browned. Optional: Broil for an additional 1-2 minutes for a golden brown top.
f) Serve the baked lemon herb scallops with additional fresh parsley for garnish.

NUTRITION PER SERVING: Calories: 150, Protein: 20g, Carbohydrates: 4g, Dietary Fiber: 0.5g, Fat: 7g, Sodium: 400mg

TIPS: Serve the scallops over a bed of wild rice or pasta.

- Add a splash of white wine to the lemon herb mixture for extra flavor.
- Experiment with different herbs such as tarragon or chives.

Coconut Curry Shrimp

INGREDIENTS:

1 pound large shrimp (peeled and deveined), 1 can (14 ounces) coconut milk, 2 tablespoons red curry paste, 1 tablespoon vegetable oil, 1 onion (finely chopped), 2 bell peppers (thinly sliced), 1 zucchini (sliced), 2 cloves garlic (minced), 1 tablespoon fresh ginger (grated), 1 tablespoon soy sauce, 1 tablespoon fish sauce, 1 tablespoon brown sugar, Fresh cilantro for garnish, Cooked rice for serving

Servings: 4

Cooking Time: 15 minutes

DIRECTIONS:

a) In a wok or large skillet, heat vegetable oil over medium heat.
b) Add chopped onion and sauté until translucent.
c) Stir in minced garlic and grated ginger, and cook for an additional 1-2 minutes.
d) Add red curry paste to the wok and cook for 1 minute, stirring constantly.
e) Pour in coconut milk, soy sauce, fish sauce, and brown sugar. Stir to combine.
f) Add sliced bell peppers and zucchini to the coconut curry mixture. Simmer for 5-7 minutes or until the vegetables are tender.
g) Add the peeled and deveined shrimp to the wok, cooking for an additional 3-5 minutes or until the shrimp are cooked through. Serve the coconut curry shrimp over cooked rice. Garnish with fresh cilantro.

NUTRITION PER SERVING: Calories: 300, Protein: 25g, Carbohydrates: 15g, Dietary Fiber: 3g, Fat: 18g, Sodium: 800mg

TIPS: Add sliced bamboo shoots or water chestnuts for added texture.

● Serve with a side of naan bread or roti.

Lime Cilantro Grilled Mahi-Mahi

INGREDIENTS:

4 mahi-mahi fillets, 3 tablespoons olive oil, 3 tablespoons fresh lime juice, 2 cloves garlic (minced), 1 tablespoon fresh cilantro (chopped), 1 teaspoon cumin, Salt and black pepper to taste, Lime wedges

Servings: 4

Grilling Time: 8-10 minutes

DIRECTIONS:

a) In a bowl, whisk together olive oil, fresh lime juice (minced) garlic (chopped) fresh cilantro, cumin, salt, and black pepper to create the marinade. Place the mahi-mahi fillets in a shallow dish and brush both sides with the marinade. Let them marinate in the refrigerator for 30 minutes.
b) Preheat the grill to medium-high heat.
c) Remove the mahi-mahi from the refrigerator and let it come to room temperature for about 15 minutes.
d) Grill the mahi-mahi fillets for 4-5 minutes per side, or until the fish is opaque and easily flakes with a fork. Optional: Drizzle with extra lime juice just before serving. Serve with lime wedges.

NUTRITION PER SERVING: Calories: 250, Protein: 30g, Carbohydrates: 2g, Dietary Fiber: 0.5g, Fat: 14g, Sodium: 400mg

TIPS:

- Grill some pineapple slices alongside the mahi-mahi for a tropical twist.
- Serve over a bed of quinoa or with a side of rice.
- Garnish with additional fresh cilantro before serving for a burst of color.

Lemon Garlic Baked Salmon

INGREDIENTS:

4 salmon fillets, 3 tablespoons olive oil, 2 tablespoons fresh lemon juice, 2 teaspoons lemon zest, 3 cloves garlic (minced), 1 teaspoon dried oregano, Salt and black pepper to taste, Fresh parsley for garnish, Lemon wedges for serving

Servings: 4

Baking Time: 12-15 minutes

DIRECTIONS:

a) Preheat the oven to 375°F (190°C).
b) Place the salmon fillets on a baking sheet lined with parchment paper.
c) In a bowl, whisk together olive oil, fresh lemon juice, lemon zest (minced) garlic, dried oregano, salt, and black pepper.
d) Pour the lemon garlic mixture over the salmon fillets, ensuring they are well-coated.
e) Optional: Sprinkle additional dried oregano on top for extra flavor.
f) Bake in the preheated oven for 12-15 minutes, or until the salmon is cooked through and flakes easily with a fork. Optional: Broil for an additional 1-2 minutes for a golden brown top.
g) Garnish with fresh parsley and serve with lemon wedges.

NUTRITION PER SERVING: Calories: 300, Protein: 30g, Carbohydrates: 2g, Dietary Fiber: 0.5g, Fat: 18g, Sodium: 400mg

TIPS: Serve the lemon garlic baked salmon over a bed of quinoa, couscous, or steamed vegetables.

● Drizzle extra lemon juice over the fish just before serving for a burst of freshness.

SANDWICH

86. Turkey and Avocado Wrap

87. Grilled Chicken and Pesto Panini

88. Salmon Salad Lettuce Wraps

89. Egg Salad Sandwich

90. Caprese Sandwich with Balsamic Glaze

91. Mediterranean Veggie Wrap

92. Cucumber and Cream Cheese Sandwich

93. Roasted Turkey and Hummus Wrap

94. Whole Grain Bread Open-Faced Sandwich

95. Shrimp and Avocado Lettuce Wraps

96. Tomato and Mozzarella Sandwich with Basil Pesto

Turkey and Avocado Wrap

INGREDIENTS:

4 large whole wheat or spinach tortillas, 1 pound sliced turkey breast, 2 avocados (sliced), 1 cup cherry tomatoes (halved), ½ cup red onion (thinly sliced), 1 cup lettuce (shredded), 4 tablespoons Greek yogurt or mayonnaise, Salt and black pepper to taste

Servings: 4

Preparation Time: 15 minutes

DIRECTIONS:

a) Lay out the tortillas on a clean surface.
b) Spread 1 tablespoon of Greek yogurt or mayonnaise over each tortilla.
c) Place an even layer of sliced turkey on each tortilla.
d) Arrange avocado slices, cherry tomatoes, red onion, and shredded lettuce on top of the turkey.
e) Season with salt and black pepper to taste.
f) Fold in the sides of the tortilla and then roll it up tightly from the bottom to create a wrap.
g) Optional: Secure the wraps with toothpicks or wrap them in parchment paper for easy handling.
h) Slice the wraps in half diagonally before serving.

NUTRITION PER SERVING: Calories: 400, Protein: 25g, Carbohydrates: 35g, Dietary Fiber: 8g, Fat: 20g, Sodium: 600mg

TIPS: Customize the wraps with your favorite condiments or spreads.

- Add a sprinkle of feta cheese or shredded cheddar for extra flavor.
- Include a handful of alfalfa sprouts or baby spinach for added freshness.
- Serve with a side of carrot sticks, cucumber slices, or a small salad.

Grilled Chicken and Pesto Panini

INGREDIENTS:

4 boneless, skinless chicken breasts, 4 ciabatta rolls or any bread of your choice, ½ cup pesto sauce, 1 cup baby spinach leaves, 1 cup sun-dried tomatoes (sliced), 1 cup mozzarella cheese, 2 tablespoons olivc oil

Servings: 4

Grilling Time: 10-12 minutes

DIRECTIONS:

a) Preheat the grill to medium-high heat. Season the chicken breasts with salt and black pepper.
b) Grill the chicken breasts for 5-6 minutes per side, or until fully cooked and grill marks appear. Remove from the grill and let them rest for a few minutes before slicing. Slice the ciabatta rolls in half horizontally. Spread pesto sauce on the inside of each roll.
c) On the bottom half of each roll, layer grilled chicken slices, baby spinach leaves, sun-dried tomatoes, and shredded mozzarella cheese. Place the top half of the rolls on the filling to create sandwiches. Brush the outer sides of the rolls with olive oil.
d) Grill the paninis on the preheated grill for 2-3 minutes per side, or until the bread is toasted, and the cheese is melted. Remove from the grill, slice the paninis in half diagonally, and serve.

NUTRITION PER SERVING: Calories: 500, Protein: 35g, Carbohydrates: 30g, Dietary Fiber: 4g, Fat: 28g, Sodium: 800mg

TIPS: Use a panini press or a stovetop grill pan if you don't have an outdoor grill.

● Experiment with different cheese varieties like provolone or gouda.

Salmon Salad Lettuce Wraps

INGREDIENTS:

1 pound cooked salmon (flaked), ½ cup Greek yogurt or mayonnaise, 2 tablespoons Dijon mustard, 1 tablespoon lemon juice, ¼ cup red onion (finely chopped), ¼ cup celery (finely chopped), 2 tablespoons fresh dill (chopped), Salt and black pepper to taste, Butter lettuce leaves for wrapping (sliced) cucumber and cherry tomatoes for garnish

Servings: 4

Preparation Time: 15 minutes

DIRECTIONS:

a) In a bowl, combine the flaked cooked salmon, Greek yogurt or mayonnaise, Dijon mustard, lemon juice, red onion, celery, and chopped fresh dill. Mix well.
b) Season the salmon salad with salt and black pepper to taste. Adjust the quantities to your preference.
c) Spoon the salmon salad onto individual butter lettuce leaves, creating wraps.
d) Garnish with sliced cucumber and cherry tomatoes.
e) Serve immediately.

NUTRITION PER SERVING: Calories: 250, Protein: 30g, Carbohydrates: 5g, Dietary Fiber: 1g, Fat: 12g, Sodium: 400mg

TIPS: Add a squeeze of fresh lemon juice over the wraps just before serving.

● Include a sprinkle of chopped almonds or walnuts for added crunch.
● Mix in diced avocado for creaminess.
● Serve with a side of mixed greens or a simple cucumber salad.

Whole Grain Bread Egg Salad Sandwich

INGREDIENTS:

6 hard-boiled eggs (peeled and chopped), ½ cup mayonnaise, 1 tablespoon Dijon mustard, 2 tablespoons fresh chives (chopped), Salt and black pepper to taste, 8 slices whole grain bread, Lettuce leaves for topping, Tomato slices for topping

Servings: 4

Preparation Time: 15 minutes

DIRECTIONS:

a) In a bowl, combine the chopped hard-boiled eggs, mayonnaise, Dijon mustard, and fresh chives. Mix well.
b) Season the egg salad with salt and black pepper to taste. Toast the slices of whole grain bread if desired.
c) Spread a generous portion of the egg salad onto four slices of bread.
d) Top each with lettuce leaves and tomato slices.
e) Place the remaining slices of bread on top to create sandwiches.
f) Optional: Secure the sandwiches with toothpicks or cut them in half diagonally for serving.
g) Serve the whole grain bread egg salad sandwiches immediately.

NUTRITION PER SERVING: Calories: 350, Protein: 15g, Carbohydrates: 25g, Dietary Fiber: 5g, Fat: 20g, Sodium: 500mg

TIPS: Include finely chopped celery or red onion for added crunch.

● Mix in a teaspoon of pickle relish for a tangy twist.

Caprese Sandwich with Balsamic Glaze

INGREDIENTS:

4 ciabatta rolls or any bread of your choice, 2 large tomatoes (thinly sliced), 1 pound fresh mozzarella cheese (sliced), Fresh basil leaves, Balsamic glaze (store-bought or homemade), Extra virgin olive oil, Salt and black pepper to taste

Servings: 4

Preparation Time: 15 minutes

DIRECTIONS:

a) Cut the ciabatta rolls in half horizontally.
b) On the bottom half of each roll, layer slices of tomato, fresh mozzarella, and fresh basil leaves.
c) Drizzle balsamic glaze and extra virgin olive oil over the layers.
d) Season with salt and black pepper to taste.
e) Place the top half of the rolls on the filling to create sandwiches.
f) Optional: Secure the sandwiches with toothpicks or wrap them in parchment paper for easy handling.
g) Serve the Caprese sandwiches immediately.

NUTRITION PER SERVING: Calories: 450, Protein: 20g, Carbohydrates: 40g, Dietary Fiber: 2g, Fat: 25g, Sodium: 600mg

TIPS: Use a good-quality balsamic glaze for the best flavor.

● Add a drizzle of honey for sweetness, if desired.
● Toast the ciabatta rolls before assembling them for added texture.
● Include a handful of arugula or spinach for a peppery kick.

Mediterranean Veggie Wrap

INGREDIENTS:

4 whole wheat wraps or tortillas, 1 cup hummus, 1 cup cucumber (thinly sliced), 1 cup cherry tomatoes (halved), 1 cup Kalamata olives (sliced), 1 cup red bell pepper (thinly sliced), ½ cup red onion (thinly sliced), 1 cup feta cheese (crumbled), Fresh parsley for garnish, Olive oil for drizzling, Salt and black pepper to taste

Servings: 4

Preparation Time: 15 minutes

DIRECTIONS:

a) Lay out the whole wheat wraps or tortillas on a clean surface.
b) Spread a generous layer of hummus over each wrap.
c) Evenly distribute cucumber slices, cherry tomatoes, Kalamata olives, red bell pepper, red onion, and crumbled feta cheese over the hummus.
d) Drizzle olive oil over the veggies and season with salt and black pepper to taste.
e) Garnish with fresh parsley.
f) Fold in the sides of each wrap and then roll them up tightly from the bottom to create wraps.
g) Optional: Secure the wraps with toothpicks or wrap them in parchment paper for easy handling.
h) Slice the wraps in half diagonally before serving.

NUTRITION PER SERVING: Calories: 400, Protein: 15g, Carbohydrates: 40g, Dietary Fiber: 8g, Fat: 20g, Sodium: 900mg

TIPS: Include sliced artichoke hearts or roasted red peppers for variety.

● Serve with a side of tzatziki sauce for dipping.

Cucumber and Cream Cheese Sandwich

INGREDIENTS:

8 slices whole grain bread, 1 cup cucumber (thinly sliced), 1 cup cream cheese (softened), Fresh dill (chopped), Salt and black pepper to taste

Servings: 4

Preparation Time: 10 minutes

DIRECTIONS:

a) Lay out the slices of whole-grain bread on a clean surface.
b) Spread a generous layer of softened cream cheese on one side of each slice.
c) Arrange thinly sliced cucumber evenly over half of the bread slices.
d) Sprinkle chopped fresh dill over the cucumber.
e) Season with salt and black pepper to taste.
f) Place the remaining slices of bread, cream cheese side down, on top to create sandwiches.
g) Optional: Cut the sandwiches into desired shapes, such as triangles or rectangles.
h) Serve the cucumber and cream cheese sandwiches immediately.

NUTRITION PER SERVING: Calories: 350, Protein: 10g, Carbohydrates: 40g, Dietary Fiber: 8g, Fat: 18g, Sodium: 400mg

TIPS: Add a sprinkle of lemon zest or a squeeze of lemon juice for a citrusy twist.

● Include thinly sliced radishes for added crunch.
● Substitute chive cream cheese for a different flavor.
● Serve with a side of mixed greens or a bowl of soup.

Roasted Turkey and Hummus Wrap

INGREDIENTS:

4 whole wheat wraps or tortillas, 1 pound roasted turkey breast (thinly sliced), 1 cup hummus, 1 cup baby spinach leaves, 1 cup cucumber (thinly sliced), ½ cup red onion (thinly sliced), ½ cup cherry tomatoes (halved), Salt and black pepper to taste, Olive oil for drizzling (optional)

Servings: 4

Preparation Time: 15 minutes

DIRECTIONS:

a) Lay out the whole wheat wraps or tortillas on a clean surface.
b) Spread a generous layer of hummus over each wrap.
c) Arrange slices of roasted turkey on top of the hummus.
d) Evenly distribute baby spinach leaves, cucumber slices, red onion, and cherry tomatoes over the turkey.
e) Season with salt and black pepper to taste.
f) Optional: Drizzle olive oil over the veggies for extra flavor.
g) Fold in the sides of each wrap and then roll them up tightly from the bottom to create wraps.
h) Optional: Secure the wraps with toothpicks or wrap them in parchment paper for easy handling.
i) Slice the wraps in half diagonally before serving.

NUTRITION PER SERVING: Calories: 400, Protein: 30g, Carbohydrates: 35g, Dietary Fiber: 8g, Fat: 18g, Sodium: 800mg

TIPS: Add a spread of mustard or tzatziki sauce for extra flavor.

● Include sliced avocado for creaminess.

Whole Grain Bread Open-Faced Sandwich

INGREDIENTS:

4 slices whole grain bread, 1 cup hummus, 1 cup cherry tomatoes (halved), ½ cucumber (thinly sliced), ¼ cup red onion (thinly sliced), ¼ cup feta cheese (crumbled), Fresh parsley (chopped), Olive oil for drizzling (optional), Salt and black pepper to taste, basil leaves to garnish

Servings: 4

Preparation Time: 15 minutes

DIRECTIONS:

a)   Toast the slices of whole grain bread if desired.
b)   Spread a generous layer of hummus on each slice of bread.
c)   Arrange halved cherry tomatoes (thinly sliced) cucumber, and red onion over the hummus.
d)   Sprinkle crumbled feta cheese over the vegetables.
e)   Season with salt and black pepper to taste.
f)   Optional: Drizzle olive oil over the top for extra flavor.
g)   Garnish with chopped fresh parsley and fresh basil leaves.
h)   Serve the whole grain bread open-faced sandwiches immediately.

NUTRITION PER SERVING: Calories: 300, Protein: 10g, Carbohydrates: 35g, Dietary Fiber: 8g, Fat: 15g, Sodium: 500mg

TIPS: Add sliced Kalamata olives for a Mediterranean twist.

● Include a sprinkle of za'atar or dried oregano for extra flavor.
● Substitute goat cheese or mozzarella for feta if preferred.
● Top with a handful of arugula or spinach for added freshness.

Shrimp and Avocado Lettuce Wraps

INGREDIENTS:

1 pound large shrimp (peeled and deveined), 1 tablespoon olive oil, 1 teaspoon smoked paprika, 1 teaspoon garlic powder, Salt and black pepper to taste, 1 avocado (sliced), 1 cup cherry tomatoes (halved), ¼ cup red onion (finely chopped), ¼ cup cilantro (chopped), Juice of 1 lime, Butter lettuce leaves for wrapping,

Servings: 4

Cooking Time: 5 minutes

DIRECTIONS:

a) In a bowl, toss the peeled and deveined shrimp with olive oil, smoked paprika, garlic powder, salt, and black pepper until evenly coated.
b) Heat a skillet over medium-high heat. Cook the seasoned shrimp for 2-3 minutes per side or until they are opaque and cooked through.
c) In a separate bowl, combine sliced avocado, cherry tomatoes, red onion (chopped) cilantro, and lime juice. Gently toss to mix.
d) Place a few shrimp on each butter lettuce leaf.
e) Spoon the avocado and tomato mixture over the shrimp.
f) Serve the shrimp and avocado lettuce wraps immediately.

NUTRITION PER SERVING: Calories: 250, Protein: 20g, Carbohydrates: 10g, Dietary Fiber: 5g, Fat: 15g, Sodium: 300mg

TIPS: Drizzle with hot sauce or sriracha for extra heat.

● Include a scoop of quinoa or rice for added substance.
● Garnish with a wedge of lime for an additional burst of citrus flavor.

Tomato and Mozzarella Sandwich with Basil Pesto

INGREDIENTS:

8 slices whole grain bread, 1 cup fresh mozzarella (sliced), 2 large tomatoes (sliced), Fresh basil leaves, 4 tablespoons basil pesto (store-bought or homemade), Salt and black pepper to taste, Olive oil for drizzling (optional),

Servings: 4

Preparation Time: 15 minutes

DIRECTIONS:

a) Lay out the slices of whole-grain bread on a clean surface.
b) Spread a tablespoon of basil pesto on one side of each slice.
c) On half of the bread slices, layer slices of fresh mozzarella, tomato, and fresh basil leaves.
d) Season with salt and black pepper to taste.
e) Top with the remaining slices of bread, pesto side down, to create sandwiches.
f) Optional: Drizzle olive oil over the top for extra flavor.
g) Optional: Secure the sandwiches with toothpicks or wrap them in parchment paper for easy handling.
h) Slice the sandwiches in half diagonally before serving.

NUTRITION PER SERVING: Calories: 400, Protein: 15g, Carbohydrates: 35g, Dietary Fiber: 8g, Fat: 20g, Sodium: 600mg

TIPS: Add a drizzle of balsamic glaze for extra sweetness.

- Include a handful of arugula or spinach for a peppery kick.
- Toast the sandwiches in a panini press for a warm, crispy texture.

4-WEEK MEAL PLAN

This meal plan is a compilation of Galveston diet recipes in this cookbook. Here we bring together the recipes introduced in the previous chapters to create breakfast, lunch, and dinner eating plan that harmonize with the essence of the Galveston Diet.

DAY	BREAKFAST	LUNCH	SNACK	DINNER
Week 1				
1	Wild Rice and Pecan Salad	Kale and White Bean Stew	Citrus Sunrise Smoothie	Pan-Seared Halibut with Tomato Basil Relish
2	Cannellini Bean and Tuna Salad	Avocado and Tomato Caprese Salad	Baked Lemon Herb Scallops	Turkey and Avocado Wrap
3	Protein Power Smoothie	Edamame and Quinoa Bowl	Cucumber and Tomato Greek Salad	Garlic Herb Grilled Lamb Chops
4	Kamut Grain and Vegetable Curry	Lemon Garlic Baked Salmon	Mediterranean Veggie Wrap	Vegetable and Lentil Soup
5	Berry Blast Smoothie	Caprese Sandwich with Balsamic Glaze	Lime Cilantro Grilled Mahi-Mahi	Adzuki Bean and Sweet Potato Curry
6	Pesto Grilled Chicken Skewers	Quinoa and Vegetable Stew	Oatmeal Breakfast Bowl	Broccoli and Walnut Quinoa Salad
7	Turmeric Carrot Ginger Soup	Coconut Curry Shrimp	White Bean and Roasted Veg Wrap	Balsamic Glazed Pork Tenderloin
Week 2				
1	Avocado Berry Burst Smoothie	Mung Bean Salad with Cilantro-Lime Dressing		Roasted Vegetable Frittata
2	Egg Salad Sandwich	Spiced Chicken Kabobs		Tomato Basil Soup with Chickpeas
3	Spinach and Strawberry	Black Bean and Avocado Salad		Sorghum Buddha Bowl

		Salad			
	4	Spinach and Turkey Meatball Soup	Millet and Spinach Stuffed Peppers		Garlic Rosemary Pork Chops
	5	Lima Bean and Tomato Salad	Tropical Paradise Smoothie		Lemon Dill Roasted Chicken Drumsticks
	6	Shrimp and Avocado Lettuce Wraps	Lentil and Mushroom Stew		Cajun Blackened Catfish
	7	Roasted Vegetable Frittata	Rosemary Garlic Roast Beef		Buckwheat Groats and Chickpea Salad
Week 3					
	1	Roasted Turkey and Hummus	Hummus and Veggie Wrap	Lemon Dill Baked Snapper	Baked Garlic Parmesan Turkey Meatballs
	2	Butternut Squash and Apple Soup	Minty Melon Smoothie	Grilled Chicken and Pesto Panini	Freekeh Pilaf with Pistachios
	3	Lima Bean and Tomato Salad	Mediterranean Turkey Burgers	Chicken and Spinach Soup	Sesame Ginger Glazed Salmon
	4	Barley and Mushroom Risotto	Split Pea and Ham Soup	Cucumber and Cream Cheese Sandwich	Almond-Crusted Chicken Tenders
	5	Sweet Potato and Black Bean Chili	Mediterranean Chickpea Salad	Blueberry Almond Joy Smoothie	Black-Eyed Pea and Collard Green Stew
	6	Sesame Ginger Glazed Salmon	Cauliflower and Leek Soup	Chocolate Banana Almond Smoothie	Teriyaki Turkey Stir-Fry
	7	Sweet Potato and Kale Hash	Lemon Pepper Baked Cod	Open-Faced Sandwich	Chana Masala with Brown Rice
Week 4					

1	Sweet Potato and Black Bean Chili	Grilled Swordfish with Tomato Salsa		Spiced Chicken Kabobs
2	Kidney Bean and Turkey Chili	Cauliflower and Leek Soup		Tomato and Mozzarella Sandwich with Basil Pesto
3	Amaranth Porridge with Berries	Grilled Lemon Garlic Shrimp Skewers		Kidney Bean and Turkey Chili
4	Orange Creamsicle Smoothie	Arugula and Pomegranate Salad		Salmon Salad Lettuce Wraps
5	Zucchini Noodle Chicken Soup	Garlic Parmesan Baked Shrimp		Whole Wheat Pasta Primavera
6	Cucumber and Cream Cheese Sandwich	Garlic Herb Grilled Lamb Chops		Lima Bean and Tomato Salad
7	Baked Salmon with Dill and Lemon	Green Goddess Smoothie		Broccoli and Cheddar Soup

A short message from the author

Hey there! How's the book treating you? I'm super curious to know what you think about it!

You know, reviews can be a total game-changer for authors. They're like gold but harder to find! Your thoughts can really make a difference.

Could you spare just a minute to jot down a quick review on Amazon? Even a few sentences would mean the world!

Simply click the link 🔗 or scan the QR code below to leave your review on Amazon

🔗 https://mybook.to/galvestoncolorcookbook

QR code

Thank you for taking the time to share your thoughts!

Your review will genuinely make a difference for me and help me gain exposure for my work.

Brant Grenier

CONCLUSION

In this cookbook, we've explored vibrant flavors and mindful choices, each dish contributing to a lifestyle that resonates with the Galveston diet philosophy. Let these recipes be more than just instructions; let them be the palette with which you paint a healthier, more energized you.

This diet is more than a compilation of recipes; it's an invitation to a sustainable, enjoyable way of living. Remember, this isn't a rigid set of rules; it's your personalized path to a healthier you. So, go ahead, savor the vibrant flavors, relish the simplicity, and embrace the joy of making choices that honor your body.

About the Author

Brant Grenier is a Chef of the Kitchen. He transforms simple ingredients into masterpieces, guided by a passion for exploring flavors. His culinary philosophy centers on inspiring confidence, fostering community, and igniting creativity in every kitchen.

Made in United States
Troutdale, OR
02/02/2024

17401239R00069